Environmental
Issues

HANDLE
With Care!

Open for Debate

Environmental Issues

Ron Fridell

Marshall Cavendish
Benchmark
New York

*With special thanks to Jack P. Manno, Ph.D.,
executive director of the Great Lakes Research Consortium
in Syracuse, New York, for
his expert review of this manuscript.*

Marshall Cavendish Benchmark
99 White Plains Road
Tarrytown, NY 10591
www.marshallcavendish.us

All Internet sites were available and accurate when sent to press.

Library of Congress Cataloging-in-Publication Data
Fridell, Ron.
Environmental issues / by Ron Fridell.
p. cm. — (Open for debate)
Includes bibliographical references and index.

ISBN 0-7614-1885-7

1. Environmental economics—United States. 2. Environmental
policy—United States—Cost effectiveness. 3. United States—Economic
policy. I. Title. II. Series.
HC110.E5F75 2005
333.7'0973—dc22
2004021814

Photo research by Linda Sykes Picture Research, Inc., Hilton Head, SC

Cover: Chris Collins/Corbis

Chris Collins/Corbis: 1, 2-3, 6; Bettmann/Corbis: 10;
The Granger Collection: 12, 14; Ted Streshinsky/Corbis: 17; Collart Herve/Corbis Sygma: 29;
Gustavo Gilabert/Corbis Saba: 31; Reuters/Corbis: 38; Photowood, Inc./ Corbis: 46;
Robert van der Hilst/Corbis: 60; Sarah Lee/National Geographic Picture Collection: 65;
Natalie Fobes/Corbis: 67; Galeb Garanech/Corbis: 94; Lester Lefkowitz/ Corbis: 99; Jeroen
Bouman/Panos Pictures: 103; Michael S. Yamashita/Corbis: 105; Reuters/Corbis: 117.

Printed in China
135642

HANDLE With Care!

Contents

Master of
the Planet

Imagine it is tens of thousands of years ago on the continent of Africa on the planet now known as Earth. But you know nothing of continents or planets. You see wilderness everywhere you look. You spend most of your life fighting off predators and seeking the bare necessities.

If you were any other species you would still be living this way today. *Homo sapiens* would be just another mammal struggling to survive in its native habitat. But you have more on your mind than mere survival, and you put those thoughts into action. You devise new weapons and strategies to catch and kill prey more swiftly and surely. You make fire to cook your meat and keep warm. You fashion clothing from the skins of animals and tools from their bones. You develop a rich language. All the while you grow in strength and numbers.

Then you migrate from your homeland. As the centuries roll by you make more of the planet your home—and you develop an attitude of superiority. You treat the natural environment as a personal possession and shape it to suit your needs and desires . . .

Now jump ahead to the twenty-first century. Earth is a wild planet no more. Satellite images by night reveal vast stretches of land aglow with human-made lights. By day they show sprawling megacities of crowded structures and crisscrossing pathways carved into the wilderness. Buildings tower where tall trees once grew. Mountains have been leveled and wild rivers tamed. More than six billion *Homo sapiens* inhabit the planet. Human activities have transformed the Earth. You are not just another mammal anymore. You are the dominant species, master of the planet!

Now what? Keep on transforming the planet, of course. Why shouldn't you?

Because you have made serious mistakes along the way. You have treated limited natural resources as though they were unlimited. You have mistreated the biosphere, the portion of the Earth and atmosphere that supports life, by dumping billions of tons of toxic chemicals into the air, soil, and water. So, now you see that some precious resources are seriously depleted and the biosphere is fragile.

What now? That is not an easy question to answer, but we shall try.

Taming a Nation

First, though, a little history. How did *Homo sapiens* manage to transform the environment so radically? Most of the transformation took place during the past few hundred years. The taming of North America began when the first English Pilgrims arrived at Plymouth, Massachusetts, in 1620. A dense wilderness of forest greeted them.

Small, scattered groups of Native Americans were the only human inhabitants west of Plymouth. These Native Americans had already made some changes to the land. They had built settlements that included land cleared for growing crops. They had hunted and fished, and gathered fruits and vegetables where they grew. But individuals had not fenced off plots of land for their own. Instead, they shared the land in common. Their lifestyle was more a matter of blending in with nature than taming and transforming it.

Slowly, the colonists cut into the forest to make farms and towns. They cleared the land and fenced it off. As they did, they seized land from Native Americans for their own, claiming that the Native Americans did not truly *own* the land, since they had not yet fenced it off and transformed it.

Over the years the colonists kept coming, and the United States was born. The new nation quickly expanded southward and westward. In 1803, President Thomas Jefferson sent Meriwether Lewis and William Clark to map a water route across the continent. Then the real job of transforming the land for human use began. Americans set out by the tens of thousands to tame and inhabit the land between Massachusetts and California.

Lawmakers helped by either selling public land at rockbottom prices or giving it away outright. The Homestead Act of 1862 gave settlers the right to claim up to 160 acres of free public land. Most of those who claimed it cleared it of trees and rocks to make farmland.

In 1877 Congress passed the Desert Land Act, selling public land west of the Missouri River and east of the Rocky Mountains for twenty-five cents an acre. There was a catch, though. This cheap land lay in an area known as the Great American Desert. To grow crops, settlers would have to irrigate the soil, drawing water from underground and diverting it from rivers. They received unexpected help from Russian immigrants who came to Kansas with "Turkey Red," a new breed of wheat for dry climates that helped turn these drylands into wealth. Soon the Great American Desert was renamed "the nation's breadbasket."

A MODERN-DAY MINER PANNING FOR GOLD

Frontier Economics

In 1848 gold was discovered in California. A newspaper of the time carried this excited message:

The whole country, from San Francisco to Los Angeles, and from the sea shore to the base of the Sierra Nevadas, resounds with the cry of 'GOLD, GOLD, GOLD!' while the field is left half planted, the house half built, and everything neglected but the manufacture of shovels and pickaxes."

Some 80,000 prospectors came pouring into California to dig and dynamite their fortunes from the earth. People came from as far away as Europe. Some were desperately poor and had nothing to lose by heading for the goldfields. Others were wealthy with families to take care of, but took off anyway, possessed, some would say, with "gold fever." Miners chipped away furiously at surface rock and sank mine shafts into mountainsides to extract the gold.

Other metals mined from the earth meant wealth as well. In 1872, Congress passed the Mining Law, which sold public land for as little as eighty-four cents an acre to companies that mined iron, lead, silver, copper, and other valuable metals. The law allowed these companies to move on when they finished without cleaning up—and they did just that, scarring the land and polluting the water with mine wastes.

Miners never thought twice about the damage they inflicted on the land and water. Historians call this attitude "frontier economics." Short-term gain was the name of the game. Grab all you can today and never give a thought to

IN THIS ILLUSTRATION FROM *ROUGHING IT*, AUTHOR MARK TWAIN IS SHOWN ACHIEVING "UNEXPECTED ELEVATION."

During the 1860s author Mark Twain tried his hand at mining silver from a claim in the mountains of Nevada. Of the gold and silver miners who ventured West, few ever struck it rich. These passages from Twain's book *Roughing It* shows the harsh economics that silver miners faced:

> **At this time, our near neighbor, Gold Hill, was the most successful silver-mining locality in Nevada. It was from there that more than half the daily shipments of silver bricks came . . .**

"Gold Hill ore yielded from $100 to $400 to the ton; but the usual yield was only $20 to $40 per ton—that is to say, each hundred pounds of ore yielded from one dollar to two dollars. . . . We never found any ore that would yield more than fifty dollars a ton; and as the mills charged fifty dollars a ton for working ore and extracting the silver, our pocket-money melted steadily away and none returned to take its place. We lived in a little cabin and cooked for ourselves; and altogether it was a hard life, though a hopeful one—for we never ceased to expect fortune and a customer to burst upon us some day.

"At last, when flour reached a dollar a pound. . . . I abandoned mining and went to milling. That is to say, I went to work as a common laborer in a quartz-mill, at ten dollars a week and board."

MINEWORKERS AT CRIPPLE CREEK, COLORADO, GOLD MINE, AROUND 1890

tomorrow. This frontier attitude is still around today, as we shall see.

In this headlong rush to clear, farm, and mine the land, there were casualties. Some were human. Native Americans were treated like obstacles to economic progress. Most were either killed or confined on reservations to make way for white miners and farmers.

The buffalo, or American bison, were another casualty of frontier economics. Hunters moved onto the western plains in the early 1870s to kill buffalo for the folks back east who paid high prices for the meat and hides. Sharpshooters armed with powerful rifles gunned down the big animals from the ground, from horseback, even from moving train cars. Experts say that herds of twenty million buffalo once roamed the Great Plains, herds so vast they looked like rolling seas of rough brown fur reaching to the horizon greeted them. By 1893, no more than two thousand remained.

That year, historian Frederick Jackson Turner delivered a landmark speech, "The Significance of the Frontier in American History," in which Turner declared the Western Frontier a thing of the past. Most of the land from Missouri to California had been tamed, transformed, and turned into wealth.

In 1930, noted U.S. physicist and Nobel Prize winner Robert Millikan looked 300 years into the past and asked himself a question: *What were the consequences of all this economic activity to the environment?* His answer was simple and positive. There was no risk whatsoever that humanity could ever do any real harm to anything so gigantic as planet Earth.

Since Millikan made this statement, scientists have been monitoring the effects of human activity on the air, soil, water, and living things on the planet, including humans themselves. And they have shown that the professor was mistaken.

Agents of Change

In 1962, *Silent Spring* was published. The title refers to the absence of songbirds, driven away by the growing accumulation of human-made pollutants in plants, insects, and water. Because the birds would inadvertently eat and drink them, these toxic chemicals accumulate in their flesh, slowly poisoning them. This process, know as bioaccumulation, happens in all living things, including human beings.

Silent Spring's author, Rachel Carson, knew her subject well. She was a marine biologist with the U.S. Fish and Wildlife Service (FWS) and she wrote with real power: "For the first time in the history of the world every human being is now subjected to contact with dangerous chemicals, from the moment of conception until death."

Silent Spring focused on the pesticide DDT (dichloro-diphenyl-trichloro-ethane), which farmers sprayed on crops to eliminate insect pests. But DDT killed not only the pests that threatened crops; it also killed all insects that came into contact with it. Most insects pose no threat to

**THE DEATHLY HOODED OUTFIT AND MASK VIVIDLY
DEMONSTRATE THIS PROTESTOR'S FEELINGS ABOUT
CHEMICAL POLLUTION FROM DDT.**

crops. Instead, they perform vital jobs in nature, such as providing food for birds.

Carson used the results of scientific studies to show how DDT worked in the environment. These studies showed that once DDT did its job, it did not just disappear. This toxic substance entered the food chain and worked its way through insects, to birds, to small animals, all the way to humans, accumulating year by year in the tissues of each. Carson documented how robins died from eating earthworms exposed to DDT and how salmon starved to death when DDT killed their food supply of stream insects. DDT had contaminated the food supply at all levels. *Silent Spring* did more than expose the dangers of DDT. It showed how human activities, no matter how well intended, can affect the biosphere in manners never dreamed of.

Environmentalism Is Born

Conservation, the movement to conserve natural resources, began in the United States some 150 years ago. The movement to control pollution is more recent. Before *Silent Spring*, pollution was seen largely as a sign of progress. The prevailing attitude was that land could not be turned into wealth without making messes along the way. Carson's book, along with new scientific studies, changed people's attitudes toward pollution. They realized it was a crime against nature and civilization. From this new science-based attitude emerged *environmentalism*. This new social movement declared it imperative that people must stop making war on nature and start living in harmony with it.

In April 1970, on the first annual Earth Day, environmental groups came out en masse to show their strength and determination. Millions of Americans across the country protested and demonstrated against human activities damaging the natural world. They delivered the message that we are living on the same planet, which they referred to as Spaceship Earth. This Earth is our home, they said, and we all share the responsibility for keeping it clean and healthy for ourselves and for future generations.

The federal government responded by passing new legislation to protect the environment from pollution and depletion of natural resources. Laws such as the National Environmental Protection Act were passed to protect the air, water, and endangered species.

The U.S. Environmental Protection Agency (EPA), created in December 1970, showed the government's new attitude

The Grasshopper Effect

No place on Earth is free of human-made pollution, not even the remotest regions of the Arctic. Toxins from pesticides, industrial chemicals, and heavy metals released in the United States travel across Canada to the icy lands around the North Pole. Scientists call this phenomenon the "grasshopper effect" because the toxins "hop" from place to place. They continuously evaporate into the air and fall to Earth again as rain and snow. As they do, they move northward on ocean currents, streams, and winds, thousands of miles from the factories and farm fields from which they came. The Arctic cold traps and preserves these toxins in ice and snow, and over the years they accumulate in the fat of animals. Scientists say that's why some newborn polar bears have become blind and weak. They have been poisoned by the industrial toxins in their mother's milk, due to the grasshopper effect.

toward pollution. The EPA was formed to "create and maintain conditions under which man and nature can exist in productive harmony, and fulfill the social, economic, and other requirements of present and future generations of Americans." The EPA reviews government projects, such as plans to create dams and nuclear waste sites, to predict the probable effects a given project may have on the environment. These predictions come in the form of Environmental Impact Statements (EIS), reports that explain how prospective developers should deal with any serious environmental concerns that may be a result of the project.

The Agents

On that first Earth Day in 1970, some twenty million Americans took part. Since then, people around the world have joined in. On Earth Day 2000, hundreds of millions of people from some 5,000 environmental groups worldwide took part.

Since the 1960s various types of people have taken up the cause of protecting the environment. These "agents of change" aim to reduce the depletion of natural resources and the pollution of the biosphere, but they have different approaches and different ideas about how this can best be accomplished. These agents of change include:

Environmental Scientists

The studies that Rachel Carson used in *Silent Spring* came from the work of environmental scientists. These scientists conduct research to identify and eliminate sources of pollutants that harm people, wildlife, and their environments. Their research involves measuring and analyzing air, water, and soil and recommending how to clean and preserve the environment. They use their skills and knowledge to help preserve rivers and wetlands, reclaim contaminated soil, design and monitor waste disposal sites, and much more.

The Media

Silent Spring first appeared as a three-part nonfiction piece in the *New Yorker* magazine. Carson's work is a prime example of how a skillful reporter of scientific facts can help make people more aware of the environment and more concerned about environmental issues. Today, magazines, newspapers, radio, television, and the Internet carry daily information about the environment. Environmental stories are an important part of today's television and print news. For some reporters, the environment is their specialty, just as business, crime, or sports is the specialty of other reporters.

Environmentalists

Millions of people worldwide call themselves environmentalists. Some belong to nonprofit groups dedicated to protecting and conserving specific parts of the natural world. There are groups devoted exclusively to rivers, oceans, birds, air, wetlands, and endangered species. Other groups, such as the Sierra Club, Greenpeace, and Earthjustice, work to protect and conserve the natural environment in general.

Environmentalists tend to blame economic forces for most of the harm. In their eyes, U.S. businesses, especially factories and power plants, pose the most dangerous threats. Environmentalists believe the business owners have a shortsighted, frontier-economics mentality—anything for immediate profit. Environmentalists feel that the best chance for real change comes through the rule of law, firmly enforced by government authority.

Free Marketers

Free marketers feel that protecting the environment should be more a matter of voluntary acts by private citizens and less a matter of government control. People should continue paying taxes to support some government control, and polluters should continue to be punished by law. But too many government regulations make it hard for businesses to operate efficiently. Free marketers feel that businesses and private property owners can do a better job of protecting the environment than government regulations ever could. Private nonprofit groups that promote this approach to protecting the environment include the Heartland Institute and the Property and Environment Research Center (PERC).

Producers

Producers harvest natural resources and use them to manufacture the products that people consume. These are the people environmentalists often accuse of living by a frontier-economics philosophy. But some producers work on reducing the depletion and pollution that result from their work. They include farmers, fishers, seed companies, resort owners, lumber and paper manufacturers, architects, petroleum producers, factory owners, and automobile makers.

Consumers

Consumers consume the products producers produce. We are all consumers, which means we all play a part in depleting natural resources and polluting the environment. But some consumers take action to lessen the role they play. They recycle paper, plastic, glass, and aluminum. They take steps to cut down on the amount of water and energy they use at home and the gasoline they use in their automobiles. They buy products made of recycled materials and eat food grown from pesticide-free crops.

Government

City, state, and federal lawmakers make rules and regulations regarding depletion and pollution and set up organizations to monitor environmental damage. Some such federal organizations include the Environmental Protection Agency (EPA), the U.S. Fish and Wildlife Service (USFWS), and the National Park Service (NPS). Each U.S. presidential administration has taken its own approach to environmental protection. Meanwhile, various groups representing environmentalists, free marketers, producers, and consumers try to lobby, or persuade, lawmakers to adopt their points of view.

International Lenders

These organizations lend billions of dollars to poor countries worldwide for environmental projects. They include the World Bank, the International Monetary Fund (IMF), and the United Nations Environment Program (UNEP).

Changing Mindsets

These agents of change all play a part in a worldwide movement to transform the way we live our daily lives. The ultimate goal of this movement is a new lifestyle for humanity, known as sustainable living.

Sustainable living and frontier economics are two very different ways of looking at the world. Sustainable living is a mindset based on long-term thinking about long-term gains. Imagine, for a moment, a miner in the 1850s putting down his shovel, looking around, and thinking to himself: *Look at the mess we're making of the land here. Dynamiting it to bits. Digging all these holes deep down into it. Dumping our mining wastes into rivers and streams and poisoning the water. Taking whatever wealth we can get and leaving our mess behind. What about the people who come after us? How can we just walk away and leave this mess for them to clean up?*

Now imagine these miners getting together, pooling a small percentage of the wealth they'd gained from the ore they'd mined, and using that wealth to pay for cleaning up the land and water. This scene probably never took place in real life because the frontier-economics mentality prevailed back then. It was the only attitude most people had. They saw the planet as an infinite supplier of resources that could take care of itself. Today, thanks in large part to people like Rachel Carson, we have a choice. We can look at the environment from another point of view. We can see it as Spaceship Earth. Cleaning up after ourselves—meeting our needs without harming the environment—is a chief goal of sustainable living.

Another sustainable-living goal is replacing renewable resources at the same rate at which we use them. In other words, making even trades: a tree planted and left to grow to maturity for every tree we harvest, a new gallon of unpolluted freshwater made available for every gallon we pollute, a square mile of ocean left unfished for every square mile we fish, and so forth.

As we shall see, many of the world's people still live by frontier economics. Like the 1850s miners, they go for short-term gain and give little or no thought to the environmental consequences of their actions.

Some people want to transform that frontier-economics outlook into a sustainable-living, Spaceship-Earth point of view. These are the agents of change. What strategies are they using to deal with depletion and pollution to bring about sustainable living? Let's take a look.

Wealth and Wild Places

Conservation brings a halt to the depletion of natural resources. It springs from a genuine love of nature. The father of conservation in the United States is naturalist John Muir. In 1867, he walked across one thousand miles of America, the first of many walks through wild places. Much of what Muir saw amazed and delighted him, but some of it alarmed him. In Muir's eyes, America's wild places were being spoiled by the relentless pursuit of profit.

Muir was most concerned with deforestation. With inefficient steam engines, railroads had to burn huge quantities of wood. Vast amounts of timber were also needed for railroad ties—one every few feet spanning the rails to hold them apart—across the nation. It takes decades to grow a tree and a matter of minutes to fell it. If trees are not replanted to replace those cut down, trees disappear, and lumber companies were not replanting them.

During the 1890s, deforestation became so severe that people feared the timber supply would run out. Muir spoke out about lumber companies and their frontier-economics mentality: "Their consciences flinch no more in cutting timber from the wild forests than in drawing water from a lake or a river. As for reservation and protection of the forests, it seems as silly and needless to them as protection and reservation of the ocean would be; both appearing to be boundless and inexhaustible."

In 1897 the government passed the Forest Organic Act, placing millions of acres of forest land under federal control. U.S. Forest Service rangers were sent to guard and manage national forests. A year later, Muir reported that the trees in Wyoming's Yellowstone National Park were now "efficiently managed and guarded by small troops of United States cavalry. . . . Under this care the forests are flourishing, protected from both axe and fire."

Nature Strikes Back

Today, federal lands are still managed by the U.S. Forest Service. Logging and mining companies and ranchers still want to use them for business interests, and environmentalists still want them left alone.

Throughout the twentieth century, federal laws protected vast stretches of forest land from business interests—and from fires. The Forest Service took fire protection so seriously that it created a nationwide advertising campaign. "Only you can prevent forest fires," the ads declared. The "spokesman" was a burly, likeable cartoon bear dressed as a forest ranger named Smokey.

The Forest Service waged an all-out campaign to prevent fires on federal lands, and people accepted a no-burn policy. It seemed like the right thing to do, and the Forest Service did it well—too well. It ignored a crucial fact: Small wildfires keep forests healthy. These small fires burn out thick underbrush and closely spaced trees. Without it, the trees grow so thick that fires burn too quickly and fiercely for firefighters to contain.

As a result of decades of this no-burn policy, massive

Smokey and Fires

Smokey Bear is the longest running public service ad campaign in U.S. history. It resulted from events during World War II. On December 7, 1941, Japanese planes attacked Pearl Harbor, Hawaii. As a result, the United States joined the war against Japan, Germany, and Italy. In 1942, a Japanese submarine surfaced off the coast of California and fired shells that exploded near the Los Padres National Forest. Would another attack set off raging forest fires? These fears sparked a national advertising campaign launched in August 1944. The first Smokey Bear poster showed the forest ranger bear pouring a bucket of water on a campfire. Smokey's image has been appearing ever since in advertisements urging the public to help prevent forest fires.

wildfires spread throughout the West. In 2002 the Biscuit Fire burned for 120 days across nearly one-half million acres in southern Oregon and northern California. The next year southern California suffered its worst fire season in modern history. Wildfires burned nearly 740,000 acres, destroying 3,600 homes and killing 24 people. Containing the blazes cost an estimated $250 million.

To Log or Not to Log

In the meantime, forests on federal land grew thicker and more dangerous. What should be done? U.S. Forest Service managers felt that certain areas of federal forests should be logged and burned regularly. Firefighters would be there to make sure that these controlled burns did not get out of hand. Then the burned areas would be replanted so that trees grew back quickly.

Environmentalists disagreed. Couldn't these managers simply step back and let nature take its course by allowing small wildfires to burn, and the burned trees to decay and fertilize the earth, while nature planted new trees to replace them?

U.S. President George W. Bush sided with forest managers when he advanced his Healthy Forests Initiative (HFI) in 2000. HFI recommended that timber companies send in loggers to thin out federal forests. The initiative was signed into law in 2003.

Instead of calling logging "logging," HFI referred to it as "fuel reduction and forest health activities." However, environmentalists pointed out that Bush's plan meant building logging roads and helicopter landing pads in national forests at public expense while the profits went to the loggers. They accused the president of using fire prevention as an excuse to pay back all the timber companies that contributed to his election campaign.

EVERY YEAR TENS OF MILLIONS OF ACRES OF RAIN FORESTS ARE
CLEARED AWAY FOR FARMS AND HOUSING.

The Woman in the Tree

The controversy over logging and controlled burning is an argument over whether nature or human beings should "control" forests. Each side presents arguments hoping to win battles in legislatures and courts.

Sometimes, though, people feel so strongly about a cause that they take direct action. Twenty-three-year-old Julia Butterfly Hill saw lumberjacks employed by Pacific Lumber clear-cutting redwood trees in the Headwaters Forest of Northern California. When clear-cutting, a forest is reduced to 10 percent or less of its original population of trees and undercover. Hill was one of hundreds of environmental activists determined to keep the redwoods standing. In 1997, she climbed up into one of the trees and refused to come down.

She had set up a living space 180 feet above the ground in the two-hundred-foot redwood she named Luna. Her strategy was simple. If the lumber crews cut down Luna, they would kill Julia Butterfly Hill. She quickly attracted a crowd. Fellow activists gathered around the one-thousand-year-old redwood, along with newspaper reporters and television camera operators. Each day she wrote letters and gave interviews. Hill stayed in Luna for 738 days, until Pacific Lumber agreed to spare not only Luna but all the trees in the surrounding three acres. After climbing down, Hill said:

I had to do something with my body to help people understand that the massive onslaught and human disrespect for the environment is affecting critical forests and watersheds. So I gave my word that my feet would not touch the ground until I had done everything in my power to protect these areas and change consciousness.

JULIA BUTTERFLY HILL UP IN ONE OF HER BELOVED REDWOODS.

To Mine or Not to Mine

Environmentalists are also concerned with the effects of mining on wild places. The Environmental Working Group (EWG) aims to educate the public on controversial issues concerning the environment and human health. In a May 2004 report, the EWG stated that the U.S. government had virtually given away mining rights to more than nine million acres of public land since passing the Mining Law of 1872. EWG member Dusty Horwitt added that "In return, mining interests have left polluted lands and rivers that cost taxpayers billions of dollars to clean up."

The Bureau of Land Management (BLM) is the government agency that grants these rights. To protest mining grants, environmental groups file legal documents with the BLM. In 2004, the Colorado Mountain Club protested the granting of leases to mine gas in wilderness areas. Vera Smith, the club's conservation director, said, "If the BLM takes a second look, they will find that the recreational and wilderness values of these lands are much more valuable than the small amount of gas that they may contain. The areas can then receive the protection that they deserve."

The BLM granted some of the gas leases, but denied others, and the battle between mining companies and environmentalists continues on about mining in wild places.

Citizens against Sprawl

In 1900, 76 million people lived in the United States. In 2004, the population passed the 294 million mark. This increase of nearly 400 percent in just over a century means that people have more and more moved onto open land—and the numbers keep growing, while open land space is diminishing.

When city planners use the word *sprawl*, they do not smile. They cringe. Sprawl is their word for poorly planned—or just plain unplanned—development. Highways, streets, houses, and businesses pop up here and there, moving out and away from cities in all directions, willy-nilly.

The result is a jumble of suburbs that occupy space that was once peaceful, open farmland. Environmentalists hate sprawl. They see it as more pollution and depletion caused by developers in the relentless pursuit of profit. But sprawl also upsets people who do not consider themselves environmentalists. We'll call them "the citizens against sprawl." As the open land around them turns to sprawl, they see their quality of life plummeting. Things grow noisier, more crowded, more disorganized, and polluted.

These citizens join environmentalists in the battle to stop sprawl. Between 1998 and 2003, for example, voters approved an estimated $23 billion in taxpayer money to fund antisprawl programs designed to stop developers from buying up their land.

The Owl and the Fly

Another disadvantage of sprawl is that it eats up animal habitat. Legal battles over sprawl may hinge on the fate of an endangered species. In Tucson, Arizona, it's the six-and-a-half-inch-long pygmy owl. The Endangered Species Act of 1973 mandated that a list be kept of plant and animal species in danger of extinction, and that critical habitats be kept safe from development. The list is updated as some species recover and others become endangered. A housing boom in northwest Tucson was slowed in 2002 when the U.S. Fish and Wildlife Service set aside 1.2 million acres as critical habitat for the last few remaining pygmy owls in Arizona.

The Southern Arizona Home Builders Association filed suit to have the owl removed from the list. Holding back development of 1.2 million acres kept land and housing prices in the Tucson area too high, the association claimed, which meant that people could not afford to move there. The case could take many years to decide.

In Tucson it's the pygmy owl. In the southern California county of Riverside, it's the Delhi Sands fly. Land in the area typically sells for between $60,000 and $100,000 per acre, as of 2002. Prices are high because so many people want to live there, and landowners want to make a profit by selling to developers.

Twelve hundred acres of the best open land in Riverside County is covered in sand dunes, and that's where the Delhi Sands fly lives. It's on the endangered species list,

The Congress finds and declares that:

(1) various species of fish, wildlife, and plants in the United States have been rendered extinct as a consequence of economic growth and development untempered by adequate concern and conservation;

(2) other species of fish, wildlife, and plants have been so depleted in numbers that they are in danger of or threatened with extinction;

(3) these species of fish, wildlife, and plants are of aesthetic, ecological, educational, historical, recreational, and scientific value to the Nation and its people;

(4) the United States has pledged itself as a sovereign state in the international community to conserve to the extent practicable the various species of fish or wildlife and plants facing extinction. . . .

which means that landowners in the dunes area may not sell to developers. Landowners complain that the fly is keeping them from making a profit, but environmentalists counter that the resulting sprawl would lower the quality of life for everyone. Dan Silver of the Endangered Habitats League in southern California says, "It's important for the long term to have some open space instead of a sea of pavement and red tile roofs."

Smart Growth

When New Jersey governor James McGreevey took office, the state had some of the worst air quality in the nation, as well as cities with terrible traffic jams. McGreevey blamed unregulated growth. "The reason many families live in New Jersey is because we have a relatively high quality of life. What we're witnessing right now is the decimation of that quality of life. The status quo is simply not working," he said.

So McGreevey turned to Smart Growth, a set of strategies to control the growth of cities and suburbs and cut back on pollution. Some Smart Growth strategies protect and punish; for example, special laws were passed to protect the banks of streams and reservoirs from new development. McGreevy also sent state environmental inspectors out to factories and dump sites to protect against violations of state laws. They found open barrels of toxic sludge, and factory smokestacks emitting far more than the legal limit of air pollutants. The polluters were taken to court and punished.

Other Smart Growth strategies encourage and reward. McGreevey helped arrange tax breaks that encourage developers to build close to existing city centers and public transportation instead of outside the city limits, and to build golf courses instead of housing developments. Many environmentalists approve. Melody Flowers, antisprawl director for the Sierra Club, says, "We recognize that the future of Smart Growth lies in actually supporting developers who are doing it right. We can't just say no to everything."

Supply and Demand

Here is one way to look at the world: Divide it up into "developed" and "developing" countries. The United States, Canada, Japan, and the European Union nations make up most of the developed world, where standards of living are high and most people are prosperous. The rest of the world's nations are on the developing side, with lower standards of living. They include Mexico, Brazil, Egypt, Nigeria, Indonesia, India, and China.

Some developing nations, such as China, India, and Mexico, are on their way to becoming industrial nations with higher standards of living. While this same process was happening in the United States and Europe, people depleted their natural resources at alarming rates. Must developing nations now do the same?

The answer seems to be yes, but at a faster rate. Why faster? One reason is high technology tools like the chain saw. U.S. farmers and lumberjacks in the 1800s did not have gas-powered chain saws to clear land and harvest timber. It took time to fell a tree. However, today's chain saws make clear-cutting possible. Lumberjacks armed with these compact, handheld cutting machines quickly make acres of thick forest crash to earth and vanish. Tropical rain forests are Earth's richest source of the woods most in demand—hardwoods. Experts say about half of the world's rain forests have been cut down in the past century, and unless things change the rest will vanish within the next fifty years.

One significant reason for this is demand from rich nations. European countries long ago nearly exhausted all their own forests. Now they are willing to pay high prices for Brazilian hardwoods. Brazil's cleared forest land can then be turned into cropland and grazing land to produce more products for rich nations. The United States and Canada want Brazilian beef, so cattle are now raised where rain forests once stood. The same is true for Malayan rubber and Ghanaian cocoa.

This is the law of supply and demand at work. If rich nations will buy goods from poor nations, then poor nations will supply that demand—at the expense of their environments if necessary.

Stopping Poachers

Consumers from wealthy countries also want to buy exotic goods from poor nations, such as elephant ivory and giant panda skins. The rare animals that supply these goods are endangered, and for that very reason there are people who will pay high prices for them—and poachers who will do the dirty work of supplying them.

Poaching, the illegal killing of animals, is a highly profitable international business. Experts estimate that animal species are going extinct one hundred to one thousand times faster than normal, and one reason is poaching. Poor nations also buy from poachers. People in Asian nations such as China and South Korea will pay high prices for items such as tiger bones, rhino horns, and a variety of bear body parts, which they use in traditional Asian medicine and cooking.

As of 2004, 165 of the world's nations had signed the CITES treaty. CITES stands for Council on International Trade in Endangered Species of Wild Flora and Fauna. These nations are concerned with maintaining biodiver-

A PARKS EMPLOYEE SHOWS SOME OF THE EVIDENCE OF IVORY
POACHING IN HIS **A**FRICAN NATION.

sity—the variety of life forms on earth. They agree that it is our duty to protect the world's wildlife, especially endangered species. The CITES signers forbid the poaching of endangered animals in their countries.

Poachers are extreme examples of people who live by the frontier-economics mentality. By killing rare and exotic animals for profit, including endangered species, poachers reduce the source of their wealth until it's gone. So they move on to another location and another animal and do the damage all over again. For developing countries such as Kenya, Peru, and India, poaching is especially harmful. These nations' rainforests attract tourists who come to see the biodiverse array of plant and animal life. Destroy the wild animals and you destroy the tourist trade.

How do nations keep poachers from harming the environment and economy? The Central American nation of Costa Rica has a history of success at stopping poachers. It began fifty years ago as President José Figueres Ferrer toured the beach known as Tortuguero during egg-laying season. Each year mother turtles dig holes on the shore, lay in 100 to 150 eggs, cover the hole with sand, and return to the sea.

As Ferrer and his group hiked along the shore fifty years ago, they stumbled onto a shocking sight. A female turtle lay on her back with her belly split wide by poachers who had cut away the tasty meat inside. After that, Ferrer worked to turn the area into a national park, on which the turtles and their eggs would be forever protected from poachers.

After a dozen years of hard work and political moves, Ferrer got his wish. Tortuguero National Park became one of Costa Rica's prime tourist attractions, bringing in an estimated $12 million a year to the local economy.

Keeping the Wild, Wild

Wild places are precious—packed with potential wealth. Besides the timber and the land for farming, oil and gas are there to be drilled and precious metals to be mined. However, most of the world's remaining wild places are in poor nations, which can't be expected to leave wild places undeveloped at the expense of much-needed income and jobs.

So, environmental groups have found ways for local people to benefit economically from keeping wild places wild. One way is conservation concessions. Land owners agree to leave property undeveloped in exchange for a concession, usually cash or jobs. In July 2002, for example, the government of Guyana, in northern South America, agreed to protect 200,000 acres of rain forest for thirty years instead of allowing lumber companies to clearcut and log them.

In exchange, Guyana received cash payments equal to what the lumber companies would have paid. The payments came from donations received by Conservation International (CI), a worldwide environmental group dedicated to preserving wild places. Currently, CI plans to arrange more conservation concessions in other nations to protect millions of acres of rain forest worldwide.

Seacology uses a similar strategy but on a smaller scale. This group is devoted to preserving the environments and cultures of islands around the world. Their motto is "Saving the world . . . one island village at a time." The group offers to improve islanders' lives if they will agree to keep nearby lands free from loggers, miners, and hunters.

For example, the remote village of Falealupo in the South Pacific island nation of Samoa needed a school. So, Seacology had the school built. In exchange, the village chiefs signed a document, called a covenant, protecting 30,000 acres of rain forest from development.

Another Seacology project helps protect the few remaining golden-headed langurs, the world's most endangered primate. Killing langurs is illegal, but poachers have hunted them relentlessly, until only fifty or sixty remain. Nearly all live on Cat Ba Island in the Southeast Asian nation of Vietnam. Poachers sell their kills of Cat Ba langurs to local wildlife restaurateurs and to people who turn them into monkey-bone paste, a traditional medicine. Seacology helps fund a project in which Cat Ba islander families protect the remaining langurs from poachers by patrolling the beaches and forests. In exchange, the families receive cash payments and exclusive fishing and plant harvesting rights in the areas they patrol.

The key to protecting wild places, then, is economic. The more value people find in leaving wild places as they are, the better the chance these wild places will remain wild.

Land and Food

The greatest single advance in human-made technology came along about 15,000 years ago when the first *Homo sapiens* switched from gathering plants to growing them. Before, as hunters and gatherers, they had to take what they could find, traveling far and wide to find enough nourishing food to survive. Farming meant a richer and calmer lifestyle. Farmers settled down. They cleared land and planted seeds to grow crops in small, planned spaces. Over the years they improved the food supply through selective breeding. They planted seeds from only the most healthful and nourishing plants and bred only the animals most likely to produce the best meat, milk, wool, and hides.

Throughout most of human history, far more people made their living farming than by any other means. Most were subsistence farmers, growing the food they needed to survive. They grew their own grains, vegetables, and fruits, and raised their own livestock for milk, eggs, and meat.

During the 1800s, the U.S. economy gradually shifted

from farm-based to industry-based, and farmers moved from the country to the city for higher-paying factory jobs. The day of the subsistence farmer in America was ending, and farms were getting fewer and larger. One farmer could grow enough crops to feed hundreds of families now, and farmers were growing them in a new way that meant the nation's soil, water, and plant and animal life were in danger of being depleted.

Feasts for Pests

With bigger fields to farm, farmers turned to *monocultures*. A monoculture is a farm field devoted to a single crop, such as wheat, beans, or strawberries. Monoculture farming makes good economic sense. It takes less time and energy to plant, tend, harvest, and market a single large crop on a given piece of land than several small crops. Monocultures also mean more yield per acre, which means more food for the growing populations of city-dwellers consuming it and more money for the farmers who produce it.

Monocultures are good for the new industrial economy but not so good for the environment. Here's why: Subsistence farms have small plots of different crops, but monoculture farms have hundreds or thousands of acres of a single crop. Certain insects eat certain crops. Armies of pests that eat a particular crop will come from miles around to feast, and monoculture farmers then have a real war on their hands.

It's a war they fight with chemical poisons. After Rachel Carson told the world about DDT, it was banned, but other pesticides remained on the market. Farmers couldn't grow monocultures without them. However, any given pesticide initially kills the insects, but gradually the species adapts. New generations build up a tolerance to the pesticide, so scientists must keep developing new and more efficient poisons. The same thing happens with herbicides, the toxic chemicals used to kill weeds.

Another weapon in the monoculture war is fertilizer. Plants absorb nutrients, such as nitrogen, from the soil. The plants in a monoculture all absorb the same nutrients, which eventually exhausts the soil of those nutrients. If farmers don't replace these nutrients, their monoculture crops stop growing.

Fertilizers do the job, but they are also harmful. In a way, they are too much of a good thing. Nutrients, such as nitrogen and phosphorous, are good for the growing crops. But too many of them can lead to nutrient pollution. When these nutrients run off into bodies of water, they cause green plants such as algae to grow in great numbers. When too many of these plants grow in lakes and streams, so much of the water's oxygen is used that the plants basically smother fish and other animal life-forms.

Animal Farms

Feedlots and monoculture farm fields don't look much alike, but they have much in common. Feedlots are farms for raising thousands of head of the same kind of animal. Normally we picture cattle grazing on the open range and chickens pecking and scurrying around barnyards. However, much of the meat we now eat comes from animals that have never roamed anywhere. Many pigs and chickens spend their lives warehoused in huge enclosures that hold thousands of animals. Many cattle today are raised in fenced areas, where they spend their time standing in stalls eating feed, drinking water, and receiving drugs to halt the spread of disease.

How deadly can nutrient pollution get? Biological researcher Antonietta Quigg of Texas A & M University at Galveston knows. She studies dead zones in the world's oceans and rivers, where vast quantities of fish and other marine life die. The Gulf of Mexico Dead Zone is the biggest in the United States. It runs along the Louisiana coastline from the mouth of the Mississippi River to beyond the Texas border. Quigg says fertilizer runoff from farm fields is probably the chief cause. Sewage runoff and nitrogen emissions from vehicles and factories add to the problem. These nutrient substances cause more plankton to grow. Plankton are tiny marine organisms that use up oxygen when they die and decay—and without sufficient oxygen, marine life dies. Dead zones range from a few square miles to more than 45,000 square miles. "Dead zones seem to have one thing in common," Quigg says, "and it's that they're getting bigger." Dead zones have turned up around the world, including waters off the coasts of Australia, Japan, China, and South America. According to a 2004 United Nations Environment Program (UNEP) report, the world's oceans have nearly 150 dead zones, and the number keeps rising.

THESE CHICKENS WILL SPEND THEIR ENTIRE LIVES ENCLOSED WITHIN FOUR WALLS.

It may not seem humane to treat animals this way, but it makes the same kind of economic sense as monoculture farming. Feedlots are an ultraefficient, superproductive way of meeting the nation's meat-eating needs. However, like monocultures, feedlots release harmful chemicals into the soil and water. A single dairy cow produces about 120 pounds of wet manure a day. That's as much as thirty people produce. California's 1.4 million dairy cows alone produce as much waste as 42 million people each day. The waste from so many animals confined in such a small space is a sure recipe for soil and water pollution.

The federal government regulates feedlots through the EPA. The new, tougher laws that took effect in 2003 require feedlot owners to reduce the amount of pollutants from animal waste released into the environment.

Environmentalists have complained that the new regulations are not tough enough. They want stricter rules in place. Some, such as David Brubaker of the Center for a Livable Future at Johns Hopkins University, in Baltimore, Maryland, want feedlots outlawed. "The way that we breed animals for food is a threat to the planet," Brubaker said. "It pollutes our environment while consuming huge amounts of water, grain, petroleum, pesticides, and drugs. The results are disastrous."

Private Solutions

Free marketers, on the other hand, do not want the government to outlaw feedlots. They don't want feedlots regulated either. They want solutions to come from private citizens, such as Tulsa, Oklahoma, inventor John Candler.

Candler invented a treatment system that breaks down pig waste, which kills harmful bacteria. It separates the waste into solid and liquid. The liquid waste is then sterilized, recycled, and returned to pig barns as clean flush water. The solid waste, now odorless, becomes farm field fertilizer. Candler's system makes for cleaner barns and healthier pigs that grow faster, which means more profit for feedlot owners.

Another private solution came from Ontario Pork in Canada, which funded a project to produce a new kind of pig. Scientists at the University of Guelph, in Ontario, genetically engineered pigs to produce what they call the Enviropig.

What makes the Enviropig unique? Most pollution in pig manure comes from phosphorous, a nutrient in pig feed. Pigs don't digest much of it, so it exits their bodies in their manure as nutrient pollution. The Guelph scientists genetically engineered pigs to make them digest twice as much phosphorous as ordinary pigs. Since these engineered pigs, with their cleaner manure, help protect the environment, Ontario Pork named them Enviropigs.

Free marketers point to the Candler system and Ontario's Enviropigs as proof that private solutions can help solve the public's environmental problems.

Trampled Earth

Not all cattle are raised on feedlots. Some traditional cattle ranchers remain, grazing their herds in wide open spaces. Some graze on public lands, controlled by the federal government. Space on public lands has always been available to cattle ranchers for a low rent. The government does this to help boost the nation's ranching economy. As of 2004, some 25,000 ranchers held grazing permits on 265 million acres of public lands in the West, where some three million cows grazed—about 10 percent of America's beef cattle.

Like monocultures and feedlots, grazing on public lands makes economic sense but damages the soil and water. On dry land, cattle trample the earth, making it hard for plants to grow through the tightly packed surface and hard for rainwater to soak in. The result is erosion from wind and water that leaves the land barren. Damage is even more severe in riparian habitats. This is the moist land, rich in native plants and animals, that lines the streams and creeks where cattle gather for water.

Members of an environmental group called the Forest Guardians are determined to undo this damage. "Livestock grazing is by far the single most destructive activity on Southwestern public lands," they write. So they are "leading the charge to challenge the ranching communities' stranglehold on our public lands—and to begin restoring our streams, deserts, grasslands, and forests."

The Guardians say that grazing so many head of cattle threatens hundreds of species of plants and animals on public lands, including endangered species. They fight back with lawsuits. Some lawsuits are filed against individual ranchers for violating the Endangered Species Act or the Clean Water Act. In some cases the Guardians try to convince the courts to withdraw ranchers' grazing rights entirely. The Guardians estimate that they have cleared five thousand cows off public lands.

The lawsuits can strike ranchers hard, even put them out of business. Some environmentalists disagree with these tactics. George Grossman is a Sierra Club official in Santa Fe, New Mexico, where the Guardians are based. He says, "They're a little too extreme. I think zero anything is not the way to go. I mean, we're talking about people losing their livelihoods."

The work of the Forest Guardians shows how much attitudes toward the environment have changed. And the Guardians are not the only group working to keep cattle off public lands. One hundred fifty years ago few people thought about the damage that grazing cattle could do. Now whole groups are devoted to undoing the damage.

Precious Water

Looking down on Earth from space, one sees far more water than land. Water covers 70 percent of the planet's surface—but most of that is saltwater. Every day all over the planet freshwater wars are waged—serious disputes over who gets access to the limited supply of the Earth's freshwater. Most of it is not available for human use. It's locked away in glaciers and ice caps at the North and South Poles. Less than .3 percent of the freshwater supply available for human use is on the surface, in streams, rivers, wetlands, and lakes. The rest is buried underground.

The more than six billion people on Earth cannot live without freshwater. Everyone needs a certain amount to drink, but that's not where most of it goes. Two-thirds of the world's freshwater is used to irrigate crops. The next largest share, one-fourth, goes to industry to help power mills and machines. This leaves less than one-tenth for drinking and sewage disposal.

As the planet's human population grows daily, so does the need for freshwater. More must be drained from the surface and pumped from underground each day. Most underground water is stored in aquifers. The Ogallala aquifer is the biggest in the United States. This underground sea lies beneath parts of eight states running south from South Dakota to Texas. Aquifers store fossil water, water accumulated from millions of years ago. Some water flows into aquifers from underground rivers and streams, but it's not always enough to make up for what humans remove. The Ogallala waters one-fifth of the nation's irrigated land. A survey of one area of the Ogallala shows that this underground sea has been shrinking at an average rate of 1.74 feet per year. How long before the Ogallala is drained dry? No one can say for sure. But one thing is certain: we are depleting its limited supply of fossil water.

Public to Private

We are also draining streams, rivers, lakes, and wetlands to meet the increasing demand for water, which makes precious freshwater the object of more disputes. Who should control the supplies of freshwater? This age-old question was first addressed by the Roman emperor Justinian in 529 CE. In his *Codex Justinias*, the emperor declared that, "By the law of nature these things are common to all mankind, the air, running water, the sea and consequently the shores of the sea."

In other words, these natural resources belong to the public—to all of us. Justinian's law became known as the Public Trust Doctrine, a doctrine that has endured. It was adopted as law in the original thirteen colonies and still applies in the United States today.

A state supreme court case from the nineteenth century

shows this law at work. Several New Jersey families charged that wealthy oyster planters were using threats to stop them from gathering oysters for food. The planters countered that a lower court had awarded them exclusive rights to coastal oyster beds. In a landmark 1821 decision known as *Arnold* v. *Mundy*, the New Jersey Supreme Court sided with the families. The decision upheld the ancient principle of public trust dating all the way back to Justinian.

The U.S. Supreme Court issued a similar ruling in the 1892 case of *Illinois Central Railroad* v. *Illinois*. The railroad had claimed ownership of the shoreline and waters along Chicago's lakefront. The Court overruled the claim. Public properties should not be sold to private interests, the Court ruled. The lakefront should be "held in trust for the people of the state, that they may enjoy the navigation of waters, carry on commerce over them, and have liberty of fishing therein, freed from the obstruction or interference of private parties."

Draining Wetlands

In these early cases the Doctrine of Public Trust ruled, but later, courts' attitudes changed. During the twentieth century, many courts did not object as state lawmakers approved the sale of public properties to private interests. Developers gained control of public shorelines, wetlands, and tidal flats and converted them to farmland, housing, businesses, factories, and landfills.

To see how this happened, we'll focus on wetlands. These are areas covered by surface water at levels of a few inches to about 6.5 feet during the growing season. They include bogs, marshes, muskegs, wet meadows, mudflats, natural ponds, estuaries, and swamps that are rich in animal and plant life.

About 15 percent of the world's wetlands were drained and converted during the twentieth century. Developers dug drainage ditches and ran the water through tubes to the nearest stream or river. The percentage of converted wetlands was higher in rich countries than poor. Both Europe and the United States drained a high percentage of their wetlands. For Europe, it was 60 percent to 90 percent. For the United States, it was about 50 percent. In the early part of the century, most drained wetlands were turned into farmland. Later, more became sites for housing and industry.

This trend continues. The federal government estimates that 100,000 acres of wetlands are filled in each year for economic reasons. Environmentalists who oppose this trend find powerful economic forces against them. Urban sprawl and the need for more factories to produce more goods continue to pull public lands into private hands.

Environmental Economics

The dispute over wetlands is a dispute over value. Are wetlands worth more to us in their natural state, or drained and developed for housing, businesses, and factories?

In their natural state, wetlands provide clear benefits. They help remove pollutants from freshwater and stabilize the water level. In times of heavy rains, they become holding areas for water that otherwise would flood nearby towns and cities. They provide homes for diverse communities of plants and animals. Migrating birds, such as geese, ducks, cranes, and herons, use wetlands as rest areas. Wetlands also provide recreation for fishers, hikers, and bird watchers.

Environmentalists point out that these natural services equal very real economic benefits for the entire community. Isn't the good of the public worth more than the benefit to a few individuals? This argument still hasn't convinced the developers or the lawmakers to halt the draining and development of wetlands. Some people point to the downside of wetlands—that they also make breeding grounds for mosquitoes that cost communities money to get rid of. Environmentalists know they must make the economic benefits of wetlands more real to the public. Somehow they must show people that wetlands are worth more in dollars and cents in their natural state than as drained and developed land.

But how do you convert natural services such as recreation, pollution control, and flood control into dollars and cents? A new science, environmental economics, has sprung up to do just that. It's a young science based on a new way of looking at the world. Can environmental economists put an economic value on the services that natural environments perform? Not until they have more information from scientists about how ecosystems operate. We know a lot about the individual pieces, such as plants, animals, clouds, and wind. We know far less about how the pieces work together in an ecological system such as a wetland.

Protecting Wetlands

Like other natural resources, wetlands can become a political issue, especially in an election year. On April 22, 2004, Earth Day, President Bush pledged to seek more money in his next budget to create and protect at least three million more acres of wetlands. Bush's democratic opponent in the November election, Senator John Kerry, accused the administration of making false promises. "[Y]ou know as well as I do, once they get re-elected, they'll walk away from that promise the same way they walked from all the others," Kerry said.

Kerry was looking back to January 2003, when the

Bush administration relaxed some of the protections for wetlands under the Clean Water Act. Environmental organizations claimed that relaxing those protections led to private owners filling in millions of acres of wetlands and selling them to developers.

Will the president fulfill his pledge or "walk away" from it? That remains to be seen. Meanwhile, wetlands have not been entirely unprotected. Some of the private landowners who violated wetlands laws were prosecuted at the state and federal level, and some went to prison. Lois Schiffer, a former federal environmental official, said, "In the late 1980s courts were reluctant to really consider environmental crime 'real' crime." But now, she said, "Judges and the public take seriously the fact that environmental crimes are real crimes and have impacts on people."

Irrigation and the River

You'll remember that U.S. farmers began using irrigation extensively in the last quarter of the nineteenth century, turning the Great American Desert (also known as the Great Plains) into the nation's breadbasket. Today, two-thirds of the world's freshwater is used for irrigation. In a way, irrigating drylands is the opposite of draining wetlands, but they both amount to transforming the environment. What consequences come with irrigation? We'll sample them by moving around the world from a river to a lake to an inland sea to an aquifer.

The Colorado River runs across the western United States and south into Mexico. At least it used to. All that Mexico gets now is a trickle. That's because the river's headwaters are in the United States, which uses nearly every drop. The Colorado is a lifeline for seven western states. If you were to travel from Nevada to Utah to Wyoming to Colorado to New Mexico to Arizona to California, much of the water you would use along the way would come from the Colorado River. The Colorado also supplies the water that runs the hydroelectric power plants that produce much of the electric power you would use.

Water from the Colorado River is also used to irrigate much of the farmland in the West. This was fine when the West was relatively unpopulated. With tons of water a day to spare, the Colorado could have easily supplied the Imperial Valley in southern California, where today millions of acres of fruits and vegetables grow on former drylands, while still supplying municipal needs, the everyday needs of the city's inhabitants.

Times have changed. Starting in the 1960s, the U.S. population shifted southward and westward, and this trend continues today. People continue to move to these seven western states. The populations of cities such as Albuquerque, Phoenix, Denver, Reno, Salt Lake City, and San Diego are exploding. And each new resident adds to the strain on the Colorado's water supply.

The booming urban centers in the West now need far more water than they once did. Add to this a long drought that began in 1999 and you have a real water crisis. More people in the West means more water needed from the river, and the river can supply only so much.

The federal government regulates the amount of water each state can take from the Colorado. But for decades, California had been using more than its fair share. The other western states objected, and on New Year's Day 2003, federal officials cut off California's extra supply. Officials also ordered the state to stop sending nearly 70 percent of its share of Colorado River water to the Imperial Valley for irrigation. Growing populations in San Diego and Los Angeles needed more than the 30 percent they were getting. Similar problems plagued other western states: too much water going to farms for irrigation and not enough going to growing

Officials at the Massachusetts State Department of Environmental Protection (DEP) use aerial photos taken during flyovers to identify and convict violators. The photos and computer software they use are similar to what the U.S. Department of Defense uses to spot enemy tanks. The software lays new aerial photos over previously taken ones and scans them to show where wetlands boundaries have changed. Sometimes DEP officials spot a parking lot or a new home where a wetland used to be. The new system has revealed that between 1991 and 2001 more than 700 acres of Massachusetts wetlands were lost that no one knew about before. The before and after photos are useful for convicting violators as well as catching them. Judges and juries can actually see the violations with their own eyes. Punishments range from fines of $25,000 to prison terms of not more than two years. Officials think that the new system will do more than catch violators. They believe it will discourage potential violators from taking the very real chance of getting caught.

municipal needs. Experts say that the crisis will only get worse as the drought continues and populations grow.

Irrigation and the Lake

Lake Chapala is a big, beautiful, blue lake stretching fifty miles (80.5 km) across the dry highlands of west-central Mexico. Years ago, it was much bigger and more beautiful. In the 1990s homeowners and hotel guests along the lake were only a few steps from the water. Now they find themselves a good twenty-minute walk from the lake, over a cracked and gritty lake bed. Today, Lake Chapala contains less than 20 percent of the water it once held. This shrinking lake is still home to white pelicans and other migrating waterfowl, along with a few surviving species of native fish, but tests show that the lake is in danger of becoming a dead zone for marine life.

There are two reasons why Lake Chapala is shrinking and polluted. One is the bustling city of Guadalajara, the second-largest city in Mexico, thirty miles north. Its more than a million residents depend on the lake for municipal water. The other reason is irrigation. The Rio Lerma, which flows into the lake, once brought in a good supply of river water, but doesn't anymore. Farmers upstream have diverted most of the Rio Lerma's flow for irrigation.

The fate of Lake Chapala is a vivid example of frontier economics. People operated mostly for short-term gain. Little long-term planning was done, and the few regulations that were put into place were seldom enforced because of political infighting between various groups. If Lake Chapala dies, people will have destroyed an entire ecosystem that has thrived for thousands of years, thus depriving themselves of a life-giving source of freshwater.

Irrigation and the Inland Sea

At first the Aral Sea's fate mirrors Lake Chapala's, but then a change—the Aral Sea is recovering. The Aral is a vast inland sea of freshwater in central Asia. Between 1960 and 2003 its depth dropped by 72 feet. Little by little, the rivers that fed the Aral dwindled. Aralsk, a city of 35,000, was at one time the main port city on the Aral. Today it is located 49.6 miles (80 km) from shore! The Aral shrank because farmers upstream diverted the river water to irrigate rice and cotton—crops that need a great deal of water.

As the sea level dropped, the content of the water changed drastically, and the Aral began dying for the same reason as Lake Chapala. Freshwater contains salt and other minerals and metals. As the water level drops, the salinity, or salt content, of the remaining water rises because when the water evaporates, the salt remains. Fish and other marine life can sometimes adapt to changes in salinity if they take place over hundreds or thousands of years, but not when they happen within a few decades. Consequently, the high level of salinity killed off most of the Aral's fish.

Suddenly the local fisherman could no longer make a living, but they were not the only ones who suffered. People living on the shores of the Aral depended upon fish for the protein in their diet. Women were especially hard hit. As they became steadily more anemic, the death rate in childbirth rose. Local populations also battled cancer and tuberculosis. Scientists believe these diseases were linked to toxic substances left behind by evaporation of the Aral's waters and spread as dust by the wind.

The Aral's recovery began in January 2003, when engineers began construction on an eight-mile (12.8-km) dike

Vietnamese farmers irrigating their rice fields

that will divide the Aral into two parts, the Great and the Small. The Small Aral Sea is due to be revived first.

Once the dike is finished, water engineers will pump freshwater from a nearby river into this mini-sea. Their goal is to flood 230 square miles (80 sq. km.) of dry seabed and raise the water level by 13 feet (4 m). This will take several years. Then, engineers will begin releasing some of this water into the Great Aral sea.

The Aral once was home to twenty-four native fish species that supplied 50,000 tons of fish a year. Eventually the salinity of the Small Sea should drop enough that these native fish will return in large numbers, revive the fishing industry, and again provide vital protein for the local people.

The Aral Sea project was made possible by an $85 million loan from the World Bank, an international lending institution. Along with the International Monetary Fund (IMF) and the UNEP, it lends money to poor countries for projects designed to boost the local economies.

As of 2004 the Aral Sea project was going well. One of its planners was Dr. Nikolai Aladin of the Zoological Institute of the Russian Academy of Sciences in St. Petersburg. Dr. Aladin said, "We wanted to prove that disasters made by the hand of man could be repaired by the hand of man. I am very proud they are building it properly now."

Irrigation and Aquifers

Sometimes people make bad economic decisions that cause them to lose a great deal of money. Nations do the same thing. Looking down upon parts of the Kingdom of Saudi Arabia from the air, one sees circular green wheat fields irrigated by giant circular sprayers. The fields stand out dramatically against the surrounding desert where almost nothing else grows.

What put these lush green fields in the middle of the Great Arabian Desert? Saudi Arabia has the highest oil reserves on the planet, which means its governing royal family has a great deal of money to spend. In the 1990s the Kingdom took a wild gamble and bet it could get farmers to grow wheat in the desert—so much wheat that it could satisfy the Kingdom's own needs and still export a hefty surplus at a rich profit.

Wheat, however, needs lots of water. Saudi Arabia has nothing like the vast Ogallala Aquifer that underlies the drylands of the area in the United States known as "the nation's breadbasket." The Kingdom of Saudi Arabia has the lowest reserves of freshwater on Earth. The six trillion gallons of water a year to irrigate all that wheat had to be pumped from aquifers through wells, and sinking a new well into an aquifer is like inserting a second straw into a pop bottle. As more wells sucked up more water, the water table dropped, and farmers had to drill deeper wells at ever greater expense. Growing so much wheat was getting far too costly, and it looked like the Kingdom would soon run out of freshwater.

The government finally saw its mistake and urged farmers to either stop growing wheat altogether or start irrigating a different way. At the time, most farmers were using wasteful circular sprayers that send water into the air, where much of it evaporated before reaching the crops. Instead, the government said, use drip systems that send small amounts of water through a network of tubes and directly to plant roots. Far less water is lost with drip irrigation systems. Today, more farmers are taking this advice, but Saudi Arabia's aquifers continue to shrink because too many people have not changed.

Other dry nations share Saudi Arabia's serious freshwater problems. The nations of the Middle East and Africa have 5 percent of the world's population but less than one percent of its freshwater, and each year as populations grow, water supplies shrink.

Transgenic Tomatoes

Irrigation is a two-headed monster. It both depletes the freshwater supply and poisons the soil. When irrigation water evaporates, it leaves behind traces of salt and other minerals that build up year after year. Sometimes the salinity level rises so high that the soil turns too salty to grow crops. Land on which crops can be grown is called arable. Each year the world loses about 25 million acres of arable land to salinity. That's an area about one-fifth the size of California. A total of 40 percent of the world's arable land has been seriously damaged by salinity from irrigation, and more is damaged each day.

This is not good news for the world's forests and grasslands. For each acre of land that is no longer arable, another acre of forest or grassland must be cleared for production. Experts say we may be in danger of running out of arable land one day. How can this vicious cycle be stopped?

There are a few hopeful signs. Scientists are developing transgenic plants to help. They have engineered these novel organisms with genes from another plant or animal that give them new abilities. Eduardo Blumwald of the University of California at Davis helped develop a transgenic tomato that absorbs salt from the soil. "Salty water is generally toxic to plants," he says, "but we have found a way to increase the tomato's ability to transport it away and isolate it from the rest of the plant cell. The sodium [salt] is taken up and kept in the leaves, away from the tomato itself."

As of 2004, Blumwald's salt-absorbing tomato plants were still in the experimental stage. Ideally, acres of these transgenic tomatoes could one day return acres of salt-damaged land to production, while producing profitable crops of tomatoes in the process.

Irrigating with Saltwater

If the salt is the problem, could it also be the solution? What if crops thrived in salty soil instead of died from it? There is one crop that does this, and scientists are developing others. The crop is salicornia, also known as sea asparagus, the world's first commercial crop produced by irrigating with seawater. The salicornia fields are on Mexico's Baja Peninsula, south of California, where the mild climate means a year-round growing season. Agricultural experts long ago pronounced this land barren because seawater from the nearby ocean had leaked into the water table and heavily salted the soil.

Scientists at the Saline Seed company proved the experts wrong. They used selective breeding to do it. Over many generations they only planted seeds from the individual salicornia plants that did best in seawater, until finally they had a new breed of plant that thrived in salty water. Salicornia is a sprout used in salads, a delicacy that sells for one dollar an ounce in the United States.

Salicornia is also grown in the African nation of Eritrea at the edge of the super-salty Red Sea. A company called Seawater Farms has built a three-mile-long (4.8-km) channel that runs from the sea into and through its farmland. The Red Sea water flows through a series of fish tanks first, where tilapia are raised. Tilapia is a profitable fish sold to fish markets and restaurants. The salty water picks up fertilizer from the tilapia waste in each tank. By the time it flows into the fields of salicornia, the salty irrigation water is super-rich in nutrients.

Ocean-Going Plastics

Now that we've moved from freshwater to saltwater, let's look at how human activities have changed the world's oceans. A Norwegian adventurer and scientist, Thor Heyerdahl, made two rafting trips across the Atlantic Ocean. During his 1951 to 1952 trip, described in his book *Kon Tiki*, he saw no signs at all of human-made pollution. In his 1969 trip, documented in *The Ra Expeditions*, he saw oil slicks on 40 of his 57 days at sea. He also saw plastic containers bobbing on the waves.

A TYPICAL SUBURBAN FAMILY ON THE LAWN WITH THEIR BELONGINGS—MOST MADE FROM OIL-BASED POLYMERS. MODERN LIFE RIDES ON SUCH NON-BIODEGRADABLE, POLLUTING MATERIALS.

During the 1960s, plastic started taking the place of cardboard, wood, and glass. Plastics come from petrochemicals, which come from oil. Biodegradable materials break down naturally over time to become part of the earth again. The petrochemical revolution has replaced biodegradable materials, such as paper, wood, and natural fibers, with plastics, detergents, synthetic fibers, and other nonbiodegradable materials.

The petrochemical revolution makes great economic sense. These nonbiodegradable materials are cheaper and easier to manufacture. They're also lighter, stronger, and more durable. Environmentally, though, they make bad sense. Instead of decaying, they hang around in their original form, bobbing along on the waves until washing up on a beach somewhere and becoming litter. By 1993, plastics made up 60 percent of beach litter worldwide.

Oceans of Oil

Heyerdahl would see even more plastics if he made a trip today. He would also see more oil. In November 2002 the rickety oil tanker *Prestige* broke in two in the Atlantic off the coast of northwestern Spain and spilled thousands of tons of its cargo of fuel oil.

Before the spill, the town of Carnota was known to tourists for its lovely beaches. The offshore waters, where two hundred different kinds of seafood thrived, supported the biggest fishing fleet in Europe. Then in came the dreaded *marea negra*, the "black tide," from the *Prestige* spill, wave after wave of it. Suddenly 120,000 people in the fishing industry were out of work and Carnota's beaches were no longer a destination for tourists.

Instead, volunteers flocked in by the thousands to help clean up the mess. They scrubbed oil off rocks and rescued what wildlife they could. Despite their efforts, an estimated 60,000 seabirds perished.

Meanwhile, oil continued to leak from the tanker, and the *marea negra* kept rolling in. Here was a case where human activity damaged the economy as well as the environment. As long as the *Prestige* kept leaking, tens of thousands of people would be out of work.

In June 2004 salvage work began. The first load of oil was extracted from the tanker, which had sunk 2.2 miles (3.5 km) into the ocean's depths. The project was expected to take months to complete at a cost of nearly $3 billion.

The *Prestige* was one of several catastrophic oil spills around the world. America's worst occurred in 1989, when the *Exxon Valdez* ran aground on a reef in Prince William Sound, off Alaska's south coast. The *Valdez* released 40,000 tons of crude oil into the sound, contaminating 1,200 miles (1,931 km) of coastline. Hundreds of

DISASTER RELIEF WORKERS ON AN OIL-SOAKED BEACH

thousands of birds, seals, otters, and whales were killed, and the mess cost $2 billion to clean up

Most of the oil pollution in the world's oceans can't be blamed on accidents at sea, though. According to one study, 70 percent comes from ordinary, day-to-day shipping operations. Thousands of tankers and other large ships carrying goods around the world routinely release oil into ocean waters. That's why Heyerdahl saw oil slicks on his 1969 *Ra* journey.

Floating Cities

Cruise ships also pollute the sea. A cruise ship is like a floating city. It must supply all its vacationing passengers' needs and wants, including toilets, showers, laundry and dry cleaning, swimming pools, beverages, and food—and that means waste. Governments have put regulations in place to keep cruise ships from releasing waste near shore, but ships don't always follow regulations.

The *Crystal Harmony* is a 940-passenger cruise ship, one of the biggest. It regularly cruises along a part of the northern California coast known as Big Sur, past a sea otter refuge near the town of Monterey. The ship's owners had pledged never to discharge any wastewater near the refuge or town. In October 2002 the *Crystal Harmony* broke that pledge and released 36,400 gallons of wastewater near the sea otter refuge.

This was one of many violations for which cruise lines have been cited over the years. In 2003 the *Norwegian Sun* released forty tons of raw sewage off the coast of Seattle, Washington. The list goes on. From 1993 to 1998, one cruise line alone paid more than $30 million in fines for eighty-seven separate incidents of illegal dumping of wastewater, oil, trash, and hazardous wastes in U.S. waters. Environmentalists say that since cruise ships are hard to keep track of at sea, far more illegal dumping incidents go unreported.

Oceans of Fish

Four hundred leading scientists from around the world signed a letter published as a full-page advertisement in the February 18, 2003, issue of the *New York Times* that read, in part:

> **In recent decades the impact of commercial fishing on ocean ecosystems has dramatically increased, and we are confronted with the unprecedented reality that we are rapidly depleting the oceans' resources. The oceans, once mistakenly thought to be inexhaustible, clearly are not.**

According to the United Nations, some 70 percent of ocean waters are overfished. Fish stocks in those waters are either falling fast or have completely collapsed. So few fish are left in these waters that they have been abandoned by the commercial fishers who depleted them of fish.

Economists have a special term for this phenomenon. They call it the tragedy of the commons. The "commons" are resources we all share together, such as the trees in the forest or, in this case, the fish in the sea. If there are no firm limits on how many fish a person may take from the ocean, then fishers will take all they can. It makes good short-term economic sense: The more fish that fishers take, the more money they make.

Tragedy strikes when more fish are taken out than nature can resupply. Then the fish population starts shrinking. At that point it makes long-term economic sense for fishers to reduce their take and allow nature the time to resupply. But in real life it doesn't work this way. Commercial fishing is an ongoing competition among different fleets. If one fleet doesn't catch the fish remaining, then another fleet will. So competing fleets travel farther and farther out to sea to fish at lower and lower depths. Finally, competition gets so intense that the supply shrinks to nearly nothing, and that results in the tragedy of the commons.

Bycatch and Waste

How did the fishing industry grow so vast and efficient that it could deplete most of the planet's supply of ocean fish? One reason is the increasing demand. People in some highly populated developing nations, such as China and India, find their standards of living rising. People eat more fish when they have more money to spend. So worldwide demand for fish is rising.

To meet it, the industry becomes more hi-tech. Improved tools and techniques increase the take. Fishing vessels of one hundred tons or more are floating fish factories, catching, cleaning, and flash freezing each day's take while out at sea. They can stay out months at a time—as long as it takes to fill the holds to capacity. New tools include sonar and satellite positioning systems, which direct fleets to where the densest concentrations of fish are.

These factory fleets catch a great deal of marine life that is of no use to them, such as seabirds, sea turtles, sharks, starfish, coral, and sponges. These untargeted animals, called bycatch, are discarded. Much of the world's bycatch comes from bottom trawling, the technique that experts agree causes the most damage to marine life and to the ocean floor. Elliott Norse of the Marine Conservation Biology Institute compares bottom trawling to "hanging a huge net dragged from a blimp across a forest, knocking down the trees and scooping up the plants and animals, and then throwing away everything except the deer." He says, "The first time I was on a trawler, I was appalled to see that for every pound of shrimp caught there were 20 pounds of sharks, rays, crabs, and starfish killed. The shrimpers called this bycatch 'trawl trash'—I call it biodiversity."

Fishing gear can't tell the difference between the target catch, such as cod or mackerel, and the other marine animals that are either illegal to catch or not worth the cost of bringing ashore. Factory fishers throw most of their bycatch back into the sea, by which time it is dead or dying. Experts estimate that in order to supply a one-pound plate of shrimp, fishers discard eight pounds of eels, flounder, sea urchins, and other unwanted marine life.

Sea turtles are especially vulnerable to fishing gear. Nearly 3,000 endangered Olive Ridley sea turtles were found dead off India's east coast in 2003. Trawlers had snagged them in their nets at the start of the turtles' nesting season. Fishers are also blamed for the decline of leatherback turtles, from an estimated 91,000 in 1980 to fewer than 5,000 in 2004.

Sharks are also vulnerable. Like turtles, they easily get caught in nets. Worse for sharks, however, is that they have a low reproductive rate and a slow growth rate. Sharks are big, sleek, muscular fish that nature intended to reign at the top of the food chain, powerful and relatively safe from predators. Sharks take twelve to eighteen years to reach the age where they can reproduce. Nature did not figure in commercial fishing nets as a predator. So many sharks are being killed before they can reproduce, and shark populations worldwide are in danger of extinction.

Exploding Water

Imagine sitting in a boat on a peaceful lake waiting for the water 50 yards away to explode from dynamite you have released into its depths. Now imagine being a fish swimming around in that lake when suddenly the water, which to you is like the air humans breathe, explodes. Shock waves turn the calm water everywhere to pounding fists that beat you senseless. And up to the surface you float, to be picked up by humans in boats.

Blast fishing is illegal nearly everywhere it's practiced, in Southeast Asia and the Middle East, along Africa's east coast, and on coral reefs off the shores of the Caribbean Islands. It's hard to stop because it's done mostly by poor fishers who work in remote places when no one is watching.

The worst blast fishing damage is done to coral reefs. Reefs are complex, biodiverse ecosystems, home to fish, crabs, sponges, and other marine creatures. They have been called the rain forests of the sea. A 2003 study showed that since the 1970s, 80 percent of Caribbean coral reefs had died, many from human activities such as pollution, deforestation, and blast fishing. Like sharks, coral reefs are slow to grow. Once a reef is severely damaged, chances of it ever growing back are slim.

Repairing the Damage

People in the fishing industry are naturally concerned about the problem of overfishing. They see their product shrinking fast toward a zero point. One obvious strategy is to reduce the size of the industry and send fewer fish-factory ships to sea. But an individual fleet is not about to cut back voluntarily. Not if its competitors continue to do business as usual and take all the fish for themselves.

Another strategy is to expand marine sanctuaries, ocean areas where fishing is forbidden by law. Fish in these sanctuaries have a chance to reproduce and increase their populations. Remember how the United States reacted when people realized that too many trees were being cut down and not replaced? Lawmakers set aside areas in forests where loggers could not cut down trees. Environmentalists want U.S. lawmakers to treat some ocean areas off U.S. shores the same way, and make them off limits to fishers.

But the idea of sanctuaries has not yet caught on in the United States. People still see oceans as they once saw forests—inexhaustible—so they are not paying attention to problems of overfishing or bycatch. Larry Crowder, a researcher with the Duke University Marine Laboratory, says, "Considering the documented decline in global fisheries, this kind of waste [bycatch] is unacceptable. But because this travesty is unseen by most people, it continues."

Farming Fish

If you visit a supermarket to buy fresh fish, you could be witness to a rare event. You might see signs announcing a special sale of "wild caught" salmon. Most of the fresh salmon available in today's supermarkets is not caught in rivers or oceans. These fish are scooped and sucked from the pens and ponds of fish farms. Aquaculture is the science of raising fish, just as agriculture is the science of raising crops. Aquaculture is the world's fastest growing source of food production. Since 1990 it has grown at a rate of about 10 percent a year.

What is it like to raise fish for a living? "Farmland" is contained in ponds on land or in pens along the seacoast. If the farm were along the coast, the farmer might live in the South American country of Chile, where aquaculture is a growing industry.

Pink buoys mark pen after pen, joined together along the Pacific Ocean coastline. Every day workers motor out in boats to feed the fish contained in the pens. Once the fish are fattened up, workers use big hoses that work like vacuum cleaners to suck the fish from their pens, then bring them back to shore.

Chile is a world leader in the production of farm-raised salmon. Consumers in rich countries are demanding more of it. In one year alone, to keep up with growing demand, Chile's salmon exports jumped 50 percent. In 2003, Chile became the world leader, producing 242 million pounds of salmon and trout.

Aquaculture Damage

Aquaculture helps the economy but hurts the environment. Fish farmers face big cleanup problems. All those hundreds of thousands of fish so densely packed together in pens excrete tons of fecal matter in tight spaces which, along with all the leftover food, pollutes the ocean floor. Then factor in all the toxic chemicals and antibiotics dumped into ocean pens to kill pests and ward off disease. Estimates are that Scottish fish farms pour twice as much waste into ocean waters as the entire human population of that nation. Scotland is another leader in aquaculture.

Farmers must also protect valuable fish from ocean predators. Terram, a Chilean environmental group, estimates that aquaculture workers have killed between 5,000 and 6,000 sea lions and other predators to keep them from preying on farm-raised salmon. Environmentalists also point to studies showing that farm-raised salmon contain more toxins than wild-caught salmon, and may be harmful to human health.

In other parts of the world, aquaculture damages the land as well as the ocean. In Vietnam's Mekong Delta, mangrove cover is only 30 percent of what it once was. Mangrove swamps, which are wetlands rich in aquatic life, run along ocean shorelines. When farmers clear away mangroves to make room for aquaculture ponds, they destroy complex ecological systems that have supported a biodiverse variety of marine life for hundreds of thousands of years.

In answer to all this, aquaculture supporters point out that the industry is still young, and like all young industries it has kinks to iron out. Fish farm owners insist that they will find ways to effectively cope with these environmental problems in the years to come.

Power for Sale

Having the power to move and carry things is a basic need of a civilized people. Earlier in human history, this power came exclusively from muscles, wind, and water. Human muscles could dig up, knock down, carry, and build; animal muscles could pull wagons and plows; and wind and water could move sailing ships, rafts, and canoes. Later, humans found ways to make rivers power mills and wind turn windmills to pump water.

These energy sources had something in common: They were all renewable. Muscles would keep working, trees would keep growing, rivers would keep flowing, and wind would keep blowing. This changed in the 1700s when steam engines entered the energy picture, powering ships and locomotives. At first steam engines were fueled by wood burned to heat water in boilers. Later, the primary fuel was coal, a fossil fuel.

Like muscles, wind, and water, wood is renewable. With careful planning, trees can be replaced at the rate they are harvested. Fossil fuels—coal, petroleum, and natural gas—are a different matter. These fuels are nonrenewable. Nature took millions of years to break down dead vegetable matter and compact and carbonize it into the combustible chunks of black rock called coal. Once this coal is brought up from the earth and consumed, it's gone forever, like all fossil fuels.

Fossil Fuel Power

In the second half of the nineteenth century, nonrenewable fossil fuels began replacing renewable energy sources. Coal heated homes and powered steam engines. Natural gas was burned at night to light up homes and city streets until the end of the century, when electricity from coal-fired power plants began replacing it.

In October 1908, the Ford motor company began producing automobiles. Henry Ford's Model T was the first mass-produced automobile that most consumers could afford. Nearly 15.5 million were sold in the United States alone. And the heart of the automobile, the internal combustion engine, ran on other nonrenewable fossil fuels, gasoline, and oil refined from petroleum pumped from deep in the Earth. In less than a century the United States had shifted largely to nonrenewable fossil fuels and significantly increased its energy output, which rose continuously all through the 1900s. Environmental historian J. R. McNeill writes that in the twentieth century alone, humans probably produced more energy than in all the other centuries combined.

Think of it: more power produced in one hundred years than in all the rest of human history, and nearly all of it from fossil fuels. Think of the freedom people enjoyed from the everyday toil of pushing and pulling and transporting everything by hand. Think of the fossil-fueled power that went far beyond the strength of human muscles. And with this sudden rise in power came a rise in the standard of living of the average American. Fossil fuels boosted the U.S. economy to new heights. That was the good news.

Coal Fires

Now for the bad news. The switch to consuming fossil fuels meant that the environment would pay a price, and so would people's health. What were the consequences of this switch to fossil fuels? Let's start with one event from environmental history that shows how high the price can be.

Burning coal breaks down into gases which in turn become pollutants that threaten human health. In London, England, in the 1950s, coal was the city's chief heat source. Londoners burned it in stoves to heat their homes. During the week of December 4, 1952, a severe cold snap hit, and people had kept their home fires burning day and night.

London was a densely populated metropolis with small houses packed tightly together. More than a million homes released coal smoke from chimneys all day and night. The lack of moving air compounded the problem. With no wind to clear the thickening clouds of pollutants from the freezing air, a low, choking layer of sooty smog fell over the city. Visibility plunged to near zero—they could barely see their hand in front of their faces!

By the time the air cleared, thousands had died from breathing the unhealthy air. The shock of all those deaths changed Londoners' attitudes toward air pollution. In 1956 England passed the Clean Air Act, which sharply limited when people could burn coal and how much of it they could burn. Not only did Londoners obey the new laws, they switched by the thousands to the cleaner energy sources of natural gas and electricity, and the quality of London's air improved dramatically.

Other rich nations, including the United States, have passed laws to control air pollution caused by the burning of coal. They have installed expensive antipollution equipment on coal-burning factories and power plants and converted to cleaner burning energy sources. Air quality has improved in rich countries, but serious environmental and human health problems from burning coal remain.

Oil in ANWR

Oil is another fossil fuel that boosts the economy as it harms the environment. We have seen how oil from seagoing vessels pollutes oceans and coastlines. Drilling for oil also has harmful effects. This environmental harm stems from economic needs and wants. Like other rich nations, the United States depends upon oil for a large share of its energy needs. Generally, it costs a nation more to import oil from other nations than to drill and pump its own, but today, the United States relies on high-priced imported oil because it has only a small fraction of the oil reserves that the Persian Gulf nations, such as Iraq and Saudi Arabia, have. As of July 2004, 65.5 percent of the oil the United States consumed was imported.

More known U.S. oil reserves lie beneath a 2,000-acre coastal plain within the remote Alaskan National Wildlife Refuge (ANWR) than anywhere else in the country. This also was the only stretch of Arctic coastline still closed to oil drilling by law. Members of the George W. Bush administration sought to amend the law and tap the ANWR oil reserves, and the oil industry and its supporters joined them, saying that tapping the ANWR reserves would reduce U.S. dependence on high-priced foreign oil. Environmentalists opposed them. Members of both sides lobbied federal lawmakers, trying to persuade their votes.

Here was a clear-cut legal battle between the economy and the environment. Supporters focused on the economic benefits the nation would enjoy if more of the oil consumed came from within its own borders. Republican congressman Richard Pombo of California was a supporter.

"The average estimate for economically recoverable oil in ANWR is 10.3 billion barrels. That is double the amount of all the oil in Texas, and almost half the total U.S. proven reserves," he said.

Another supporter was H. Sterling Burnett of the National Center for Policy Analysis, a nonprofit research organization that advocates a free-market approach to dealing with the environment. He wrote that "Opening ANWR to oil and gas development will not make the United States energy-independent, but it will reduce U.S. dependence on foreign oil, shrink the country's trade deficit and, at the same time, provide jobs, state and local tax revenue, and royalty payments to the federal government."

How Much Harm?

Opponents insisted that the oil from ANWR would not be enough to bring down gas prices at the pump. The Democratic Policy Committee, which is run by U.S. Senate Democrats, gathers and reports information about political issues. The group issued a statement that read: "ANWR would provide a total of less than a year's worth of oil supply. For that temporary and limited benefit, Americans should not be asked to develop the last pristine sector of Alaska's North Coast, a fragile ecosystem of critical significance to hundreds of species and one of the last places in America where human presence is undetectable."

Opponents focused on the harm the drilling held for the fragile Arctic soil, plant life, and wildlife. Grizzlies, polar bears, musk oxen, wolves, bowhead whales, and caribou inhabit ANWR. How would drilling affect them, and the land itself?

To find out, Congress called for a report from the National Academies, a nonprofit, independent organization of experts in science and technology that gives free advice to the federal government and the public. Their report examined the effects of drilling on wildlife, plant life, and soil in the regions along the Arctic coast near ANWR.

The academy members represented an impartial mix of viewpoints. It was no surprise, then, that their final report showed mixed results. Animals had adapted to drilling well, the report said. Noise from the drilling activity had disturbed bowhead whale and caribou, for instance, but the animals had successfully changed their migration patterns to compensate. The land was another matter. The area's harsh climate made the Arctic soil so superfragile that a tire track could remain pressed into the land permanently. Some of the damage could be cleaned up, but at a high cost. Other damage could remain for centuries, the report said.

Opponents said the report clearly showed that oil drilling would destroy this unspoiled wilderness. Congressman Ed Markey of Massachusetts said, "The National Academies' report reveals what we have suspected all along, that oil and gas exploration and development have significant impact on wildlife and their habitat and is leaving a legacy of pollution on one of America's most pristine areas."

Supporters of drilling called the report biased and unfair. Alaskan business groups agreed. The drilling was badly needed to boost the depressed local economy, they claimed, as well as to ease America's dependence on foreign oil.

In June 2004 the ANWR drilling provision was tabled (set aside) in the House of Representatives of the U.S. Congress. Roger Schlickeisen, president of Defenders of Wildlife, said: "This is an encouraging development, but those of us who care about the Arctic Refuge must remain vigilant, as energy industry backers have shown they will do or say just about anything to throw open the refuge to the oil companies."

Schlickeisen's statement shows the deep distrust that can arise between environmentalists and developers when economic and environmental issues collide. One group often sees the other as willing to stoop to almost any level to win. This distrust fuels the fight. The ANWR battle is sure to continue in the years to come.

Lead in the Lungs

Automobiles revolutionized travel and provided jobs for millions, but not without consequences. Tons of exhaust coming from the billions of gallons of gasoline burned by millions of automobiles each year has polluted the atmosphere. Ironically, the person who did the most to boost fuel economy was also the person who did more to pollute the atmosphere than anyone in history. In the 1920s, Thomas Midgley Jr. worked as a chemical engineer for General Motors, makers of automobiles such as Cadillac, Pontiac, and Buick. Midgley added chemicals to gasoline, hoping to find a way to boost automobile mileage. He found what he was seeking when he added tetra-ethyl lead. This new ingredient upped gas mileage by an astonishing 50 percent! Thanks to Midgley, people got more mileage for their money.

But they also got dangerously polluted air. Burning this new kind of gasoline put lead into the atmosphere, and inhaling lead is bad for human health. To protect its profits, General Motors managed to delay government regulation of lead in gasoline until 1970. By then medical research had discovered that most Americans had abnormally high levels of lead in their blood as a result of breathing in the automobile exhaust from leaded gasoline.

Starting in 1975, lead levels in U.S. gasoline were gradually lowered until 1986, when leaded gas was phased out. Between 1977 and 1994, lead concentrations in the air de-

After pioneering leaded gasoline, Thomas Midgley Jr. went on to revolutionize the refrigeration industry. The key was Freon, a compound made from chlorofluorocarbons (CFCs). His idea was patented in 1928. Freon made refrigeration safer, but it also proved harmful to human health. The CFCs released from refrigerators and air conditioners damaged the ozone layer in the stratosphere, which extends from 11 to 31 miles (17 to 50 km) above the Earth. The ozone acts as a planetary sunscreen, protecting skin against harmful ultraviolet rays. Scientific research from the 1970s showed that CFCs were thinning the ozone layer, thus letting in these harmful rays. As a result, the threat of skin cancer was rising. Freon was phased out in 1995, not just in the United States but worldwide, and the ozone layer began repairing itself.

Midgley's tragic life story is one of unintended consequences. He tried helping people but ended up hurting them, and finally himself as well, fatally. In 1940 he got polio, a crippling disease. Midgley used his relentlessly inventive mind to design a system of ropes and pulleys to help him get around. One day, at age fifty-five, the last unintended consequence of his good intentions took place. He got tangled up in his invention and died of strangulation, suspended in midair.

clined by about 95 percent. Leaded gas was then phased out in Europe in the 1990s.

Gas Guzzlers

Phasing out leaded gas reduced air pollution from automobile exhaust but didn't eliminate it. The problem remains today. As the population grows and more people buy cars, more exhaust is released, which creates more pollution in the atmosphere. So we keep looking for better ways to keep it in check.

One way is to drive smaller, more fuel-efficient cars. During the last quarter of the twentieth century many Americans did just that. Then the trend reversed as people chose to drive SUVs, vans, and light-duty trucks. From 2001 to 2002, sales of these vehicles rose 30 percent. Meanwhile, they grew in size as well as sales. In 2003 the average new car or light-duty truck weighed in at 4,021 pounds—the first time since the mid-1970s that cars had broken the two-ton barrier. Some SUVs even broke the three-ton barrier, including the Chevy Tahoe, Lincoln Navigator, Toyota Land Cruiser, and Dodge Ram 1500 pickup. Since heavier vehicles need more energy to run, driving means using more gas, which in turn means releasing more pollutants into the air.

All things considered, is this trend to heavier, lower-gas-mileage vehicles necessarily a bad thing? Some people think not. They argue that if Americans desire bigger cars that need more gasoline, they should be free to purchase them. After all, freedom of choice is what a democratic society with a capitalist economy is all about. If consumers choose SUVs over protecting the environment, that's their business. Besides, say auto industry spokespeople, driving bigger cars make drivers feel they'll be safer if they should ever get into a crash.

Other people, including most environmentalists, take

the opposite view. First, they point out that government data show that people driving or riding in an SUV are nearly 11 percent more likely to die in an accident than people in passenger cars. Environmentalists also feel that driving big, gas-guzzling vehicles is irresponsible and that people who buy them are thinking only of their own short-term enjoyment. We all have to breathe the same air. Polluting it hurts everyone, now and in years to come.

Environmentalists point to Europe, where people buy smaller cars and drive them less, partly because gasoline routinely costs twice what U.S. drivers pay. European governments put a high tax on gasoline. That's what raises the price. Environmentalists say the U.S. government should do the same, and use the money to fund environmental protection, conservation, and public transportation. Instead, it has been subsidizing the oil and gas industries for decades. The government routinely gives them economic breaks, using taxpayer dollars, to keep profits high. A *Washington Post* editorial from March 29, 2004, puts the blame squarely on U.S. presidents and their administrations, both present and past, for "not having had the courage to wean the country off low-priced fuel."

Telecommuting Helps

So, automobiles pollute the air and Americans make things worse by driving heavier vehicles that use more gasoline. Is anything being done to help?

Yes, several things. One is switching to telework or telecommuting. Instead of driving to an office, more people are working from home, using computers, telephones, and fax machines. For example, in 2004 one of the world's largest companies, AT&T, put telework programs into place so that thousands of its employees could work at home.

AT&T called the program a big success. It estimated that teleworkers saved driving 110 million miles to and from work, which saved 5.1 million gallons of gasoline and kept 50,000 tons of pollutants from the air. Telecommuting was good for profits too. Telecommuters tended to do their jobs more efficiently from home. AT&T estimated that they increased the company's profits by $100 million, while saving $25 million in reduced office space and equipment.

Hybrids and SUVs

Some car companies, including Toyota, Honda, and Ford, are helping by developing hybrids. A hybrid fills up at a gas pump just like a conventional car, but under the hood things are different. Hybrids run on two motors, one the standard gas variety and the other a battery-powered electric. At low speeds the electric motor does the work by itself, and the car runs silently, releasing zero pollutants. When the driver accelerates, the gas engine kicks in to help. When the driver hits the brakes, the energy used to slow the car is captured to recharge the battery. At a stoplight, the gas engine shuts off, saving fuel. A hybrid's gas mileage is significantly higher than for a conventional car. The 2004 Toyota Prius averaged 60 miles per gallon (mpg) in the city and 51 mpg on the highway.

As of 2005, the U.S. auto industry was looking in two distinctly different directions. On one side were the SUVs and other heavy, low-gas-mileage cars, which continued to be popular and profitable. On the other side were the lighter, higher-mileage, more environmentally friendly hybrids. Hybrids weren't selling nearly as well, but sales were picking up sharply. Automakers would continue to produce as many low-gas-mileage SUVs, on the one hand, or environmentally friendly hybrids, on the other, as public demand dictated.

Cars of the Future?

The hybrid is a recent fuel-efficient innovation in automobile technology. Others are in the works. The fuel-cell car runs on electricity generated by chemically combining two renewable energy sources, hydrogen and oxygen. The fuel-cell car is nonpolluting. Instead of gaseous exhaust, it emits water droplets. Fuel cells have powered lunar landers, with astronauts drinking the water they emit.

Will fuel-cell cars eventually replace the gasoline-powered variety? Some experts are hopeful. They predict the first practical models could appear on U.S. roads by 2013. Some are more doubtful. Carlos Ghosn, an executive with the automaker Nissan, said, "Today a fuel cell car probably costs about—I'm going to be optimistic—$700,000. We're far from sticker price, eh? We're going to have to get it down to $20,000, $30,000."

Others say an affordable fuel-cell car is flat-out impossible. Walter McManus of J. D. Power and Associates, a company that rates automobiles, said: "Hydrogen is the fuel of the future and it will always be the fuel of the future. In other words, it's all science fiction." The single biggest roadblock is that new factories, pipelines, and fueling stations would have to be put in place nationwide to manufacture, store, and sell hydrogen and oxygen instead of gasoline.

Some environmentalists are doubtful too, but for different reasons. They think affordable fuel-cell cars could be a reality far sooner than experts predict. But it won't happen, they say, because big oil and gasoline companies, supported by government subsidies, won't let it happen. At least they won't let it happen until decades in the future when the depletion of nonrenewable oil and gas drives the price of gasoline so sky-high that gas-powered cars would cost as much to run as fuel-cell cars.

Imagine running your car on the oil that fast-food restaurants use to make french fries. It's happening right now. A Los Angeles restaurant owner got the idea when he thought about the money he was paying to have the 10 gallons of vegetable oil he used in his fryers each day hauled away to a landfill. Instead, he decided to start using it to run his diesel-powered Ford Excursion, after reheating and filtering it first. The advantages were both economical and environmental. He saved the money he would have had to pay for gasoline, and his car was nearly pollution free. Vegetable oil is a clean-burning fuel. True, there is the odor of french fries coming from the exhaust, but very little else.

Voluntary or Mandatory?

The Clean Air Act of 1970 did its job well. Air pollution nationwide has been dropping ever since the act was passed. Between 1970 and 2000, pollution levels fell by 48 percent, even though the U.S. population and economy grew. The Clean Air Act shows that government regulations, if properly enforced, can reverse the damage of human activities on the environment.

Environmentalists aren't satisfied, though. They insist that federal standards be stricter—and more strictly enforced. Environmental groups grade presidential administrations. They gave low marks to the George H. Bush administration, saying that Bush's environmental programs heavily favored the economy over the environment. One of these programs was Bush's Clear Skies Initiative. Environmentalists agreed with part of it, the part that called for coal-powered electric utilities to reduce the amount of pollutants released into the air until meeting federal clean air standards. Reducing pollution was a step in the right direction, they said.

But Clear Skies made those reductions voluntary. Each utility was free to reduce pollutants according to its own schedule in line with its own financial situation. If they made the reductions mandatory instead of voluntary, energy prices for consumers would shoot up, the Bush administration said.

Environmentalists were outraged. Giving these polluting utilities choices was the same as letting them off the hook, they said. Left to their own devices, utility companies would be ruled by the same frontier-economics mentality they had always been ruled by. They would not spend money on new, hi-tech equipment to reduce pollution unless they had to, and the nation's air pollution levels would remain high. Bush's opponents in Congress agreed. Senator John Edwards of North Carolina said, "The Bush administration doesn't want people to see what these rules would do because they are afraid of the truth. President Bush's gift to polluters promises more smog, more soot, and more premature deaths."

Small Habit Changes

Individual cities and states also have clean air goals to meet. As of April 2004, more than half the U.S. population lived in and around areas that violated federal clean air standards, and some of these violations could be serious enough to endanger human health. For example, some five hundred counties were in violation of ozone standards. The result was smog, a mix of ozone and soot that can accumulate in lungs and cause heart attacks and premature death. The government may punish areas that violate these standards by holding back federal money for building and maintaining roads. Or it may stop new industries from locating in these areas, which would hurt the local economy.

Some cities have taken action to stay off the violators' list. In San Antonio, Texas, factories, schools, and businesses joined in a city-wide effort to reduce pollution. Petroleum refineries reformulated the gasoline they produced to help lower automobile pollution. Companies urged employees to bring their lunches and eat in company cafeterias instead of driving to lunch in cars. Businesses with drive-through lanes asked customers to come inside instead of waiting in line with their motors running. San Antonio school districts changed the schedules to help reduce their need for air conditioning and electricity. They also helped organize groups of parents living near schools to take turns walking students to and from school instead of driving.

Dorothy Birch is a local government official. She said, "We are looking for small habit changes that people can keep up over a lifetime. There is no crumb too small." San Antonio city officials believe all these small changes helped keep them off the violators' list and helped attract an $800 million Toyota plant to San Antonio in 2003. The chief competitor for the factory, Dallas, was on the list.

Make Polluters Pay

Finally, the most direct method to reduce air pollution is to make the polluters themselves pay. Governor Ed Rendell of Pennsylvania liked this idea. He saw it as a way of boosting the state's economy and funding new state environmental protection programs. The usual way to fund these programs was through a tax hike on state residents. Instead, Rendell raised the dumping fees at state landfills and began charging utilities and factories for every pound of toxic chemicals they emitted.

The money from these new fees would help pay for state parks, help preserve farmland from development, clean up polluted industrial sites and abandoned mines, and fund mass transit. Governor Rendell said, "If we can make our cities and towns more livable, offer sportsmen clean streams and healthy game lands, respond to growing needs to preserve farmland and open space and to repair the environmental damage of our industrial past, Pennsylvania will be a more attractive place for families and employers to come and to stay."

Liquid Power

Hydroelectric power is one of the cheapest and cleanest forms of human-made energy. A hydroelectric power plant uses running water to turn a turbine propeller. The spinning turbine turns a metal shaft in an electric generator, which is the motor that produces the electricity. Nothing is burned. No pollutants foul the air.

But hydroelectric power does involve transforming the environment. Harnessing the power of running water means reshaping the land. Wild rivers must be dammed to build up a constant water supply. Sometimes this means changing the natural courses of rivers and building up mammoth reservoirs by putting thousands of acres of land underwater. Several million dams were built during the last century. By the 1990's about two-thirds of the world's stream flow passed over or through dams.

Sometimes people living nearby suffer when dams are built. China's Three Gorges Dam, begun in 1993 and due for completion in 2009, will be the largest hydroelectric dam in the world. It will stretch for a mile across the Yangtze River and rise to 600 feet above the valley floor. The total cost is estimated at between $17 billion and $100 billion. That's a lot of money, but the dam will provide a great deal of power at low cost. When the Three Gorges Dam project is finished, it will generate about one-ninth of China's total electric power.

If things go as planned, the dam could bring China rich economic benefits. A 350-mile (500-km) reservoir behind the dam will hold more than a trillion cubic feet of water, and more than a million people will become environmental refugees. With their homes and farms underwater, they will have to move to higher ground.

China's Nu River project should not displace nearly as many people, even though thirteen separate dams are planned. This hydroelectric project is slated for a part of China that is nearly uninhabited. The area around the Nu River, known as the Grand Canyon of the Orient, lies in the rugged mountain ranges east of the Himalayas, the highest mountains in the world. Environmentalists in China were concerned. They said that if the Nu River plans were carried out, future generations would have one less place left to go to see unspoiled nature. But they also know that

China's energy needs will continue growing as its population grows and its standard of living rises.

Leapfrogging

In a developing nation like China, environment often takes a backseat to economy. However, the Chinese government has announced plans to reverse this trend in some areas of energy production and use. Their plans focus on a strategy known as leapfrogging. The idea is that new industrializing countries can leap over the high-polluting phase of energy development and avoid it.

How? By using new, low-polluting technologies in place of the old high-polluting ones. The Chinese hope to develop low-polluting power sources, for instance, to power the millions of new cars its citizens will be buying in years to come. These sources include gasoline-electric hybrids and fuel cell cars. The Chinese also hope to use new technologies to meet their needs for increased iron and steel output while minimizing harmful effects on the environment.

Lethal Weapons

The world first saw nuclear energy at work when the United States dropped two atomic bombs on Japan, bringing an end to World War II. Some 200,000 people were killed directly by the bombs dropped on the cities of Hiroshima and Nagasaki in August 1945, and many more died of radiation-related diseases later on. Not until the 1960s was nuclear energy used for peaceful purposes, as a nearly pollution-free energy source.

Nuclear power was relatively inexpensive, but there was always the chance of a catastrophic accident. The most serious U.S. nuclear accident struck the Three Mile Island nuclear power plant near Middletown, Pennsylva-

A Russian woman honoring the dead from the Chernobyl disaster

nia, on March 28, 1979. Pumps supplying water to cool the reactor stopped working, and after a series of accidents and human errors, nuclear fuel overheated. About half of the nuclear core melted. If it had gotten through the walls and into the open air, the results could have been catastrophic. It did not. No one was killed or injured at Three Mile Island, but sweeping changes were made to safety procedures in all U.S. nuclear power plants.

The nuclear energy age lasted into the 1980s. Then came a catastrophic event that made people think back to the devastating nuclear bombs of World War II. Chernobyl, a city in the Ukraine area of the former Soviet Union, was home to a huge nuclear power plant. In April 1986, workers testing one of its reactors failed to follow basic safety procedures. Their mistakes led to a catastrophic chain reaction. A series of explosions and a mammoth fireball blew off the reactor's steel and concrete shell, releasing radioactivity into the air. The accident immediately killed at least thirty people. High radiation levels in the area meant that 135,000 people had to be evacuated.

The tragedy continued to unfold when some 800,000 civilians and soldiers were sent in to clean up the intensely radioactive mess. Many wore no special protection beyond gauze face masks to filter out radioactive dust. The total release of radiation from the Chernobyl reactor was hundreds of times more than the radiation from the Hiroshima and Nagasaki bombs. Radioactivity on this scale causes cancer in humans. An unknown number of cleanup workers have died of cancer from this radiation exposure. Because cancer can take decades to develop, more people will die from the Chernobyl radiation in the years to come.

Before Chernobyl, many people saw nuclear power in terms of bad news and good news. It was potentially dangerous to the environment and to human health, but it was also the cheapest and most pollution-free energy source on the planet. The source material, uranium, is mined, but there are no scarcity problems, since only small amounts of uranium are used. With all these benefits, people took a wait-and-see attitude.

Chernobyl changed that attitude. The disaster gave everyone in the Northern Hemisphere at least a small dose of radiation, and the danger is not over. Radioactivity remains in the environment in the form of fallout, potentially lethal particles that descend to the earth's surface after a nuclear explosion. Some of Chernobyl's fallout will be here for the next 24,000 years.

Not In My Backyard

Chernobyl put an end to plans for building new U.S. nuclear power plants, at least temporarily. But problems remained. While nuclear energy produced power that was low in pollution, it left behind nuclear waste that was just the opposite. As of 2004 there were still 103 commercial plants operating in the United States and each one produced waste from worn-out radioactive materials. Radioactive waste can't just be burned or buried and forgotten. The EPA states, "Because it can be so hazardous and can remain radioactive for so long, finding suitable disposal facilities for radioactive waste is difficult."

"Difficult" is putting it mildly. Radioactive waste does not break down and stop being dangerous to human health. Future options include burying this deadly stuff in rock formations under the deep ocean floor, sealing it away in ice sheets and glaciers, even rocketing it off into outer space. Until we develop the technology to do these things, we will continue to bury it underground.

It's no accident that most nuclear waste sites are far

from civilization. When officials propose to build a disposal site in a populated area, they nearly always encounter fierce opposition. Social scientists call this attitude the NIMBY syndrome—Not In My Backyard. People tend to agree that nuclear waste must be disposed of somewhere, just so long as it's not in their town.

On rare occasions, economic rewards alter that attitude. The small town of Snelling, South Carolina, gets a big chunk of its city budget from taxes paid by Chem-Nuclear Systems Inc., a nuclear disposal company. Chem-Nuclear runs a 235–acre (94–hectare) disposal site there. As of 2004, thirty-nine states were sending their low-level nuclear waste to the Snelling site. Low-level nuclear waste includes material used to handle the highly radioactive parts of nuclear reactors and waste from medical X-ray machines. Low-level waste is easier to dispose of than high-level waste, which is generally material from the core of a nuclear reactor or weapon. The low-level waste is sealed tight in plastic casks placed inside underground concrete vaults, then covered with soil and a waterproof seal.

In ten to fifty years, this low-level waste will have decayed enough to be disposed of as normal refuse. However, environmentalists point out, these vaults may not be completely waterproof. Water could leak in from the sides, become contaminated, and leak back out, spreading radioactive contamination. And the Snelling site is on some of the most waterlogged land in the nation. Bob Guild, an environmental lawyer and member of the Sierra Club, said that "It's absolutely the most primitive nuclear waste technology you could imagine. The idea of burying it in a very wet hole in the ground is idiocy." Environmentalists have been trying to shut the site down for years, but the South Carolina legislature has kept it open. The state receives several million dollars a year from disposal fees.

Sun and Wind

Nonrenewable fossil fuel sources are high in pollution. Hydroelectric power alters the landscape and creates environmental refugees. Nuclear energy is dangerous and on the decline. These conventional energy sources all have drawbacks. The search is on for new energy sources that won't harm the environment and human health, and won't be depleted. Ironically, this means turning back to natural, renewable power sources that have always been available free of charge: the sun and the wind.

Power from the sun, *solar power*, is a low-cost source that can serve households, one at a time. Instead of buying electricity from massive hydroelectric dams or coal-fired power plants, a family can collect the energy it needs from solar panels mounted on or around their house. Solar power is ideally suited to poor countries where most people must rely on undependable, underequipped power plants, or make do with no electricity at all. Poor countries getting power in this way, from nonpolluting solar panels instead of polluting power plants, is a good example of leapfrogging.

World lending organizations are at work promoting solar power in developing nations. In 2003 the UNEP hooked up with two of India's largest banking groups. Together, they developed a $7.6 million low-cost lending program to help some 18,000 Indian households convert to solar power. UNEP Executive Director Klaus Toepfer said, "This initiative helps to meet both environmental and development objectives by overcoming a major barrier to increasing the use of renewable energy—access to finance."

Most wind power used to generate electricity comes from wind farms, where dozens of windmills are set high on hills, plateaus, and other windy locations. Like solar power, however, some wind power equipment has been designed with individual buildings in mind. In the Netherlands, small

A WIND FARM IN CALIFORNIA'S REMOTE AND RUGGED TEHACHAPI PASS

windmills made of lightweight stainless steel are mounted on homes and apartment buildings.

Both solar and wind power suffer from a disadvantage that conventional energy sources do not. They are intermittent. Hydroelectric plants, coal-fired power plants, and nuclear power plants issue a steady flow of power. But clouds can hide the sun and the wind can die down. Power grids, which store electricity, are built for a steady stream of energy. They aren't made to handle sudden, intermittent surges of energy from partly sunny days or turbulent gusts of wind.

Scientists are working on new technologies to store these surges of energy. One example is the hi-tech windmills used in cities in the Netherlands. They are designed to take advantage of the extreme turbulence and quick shifts in direction of city winds that are funneled between buildings and snake along winding streets. The smallest models weigh only about four hundred pounds and can be installed in a few hours.

In years to come, experts say, this trend will continue. The sun and wind will supply more of the constantly growing demand for energy more economically and with far less damage to the environment than conventional sources. But for the time being, polluting fossil fuels will continue to dominate the energy landscape.

Produce and Consume

By the dawn of the twentieth century, many people in developed countries had the chance to earn the wages to purchase at least some of the objects of their wishes and desires. Production rose to meet increasing consumer demand, while advances in technology increased output. During the twentieth century, global industrial output increased by 4,000 percent.

Here was a new kind of society based on producing and consuming. The more workers produced, the more there was for consumers to consume. In rich countries such as the United States, people responded by working harder to afford more consumer goods. During the twentieth century millions of Americans acquired luxuries of wealth and comfort that lay beyond their ancestors' wildest dreams. They bought houses with indoor plumbing and central heating. They bought cars and radios and washing machines and refrigerators and more.

Ford Gets Consumers Rolling

Some historians and economists call December 1, 1913, the birthday of the modern consumer society. On that day Henry Ford's moving assembly line came to life. Now cars could be made faster and at lower cost. Ford realized that the better off his workers were, the more profits he would make. So he made sure they could afford to buy the cars they were producing. At one point one of his Model T cars could be purchased for as little as $280. In today's money, that would be about $3000. Ford's workers were among the many consumers who bought his automobiles during the early years of production.

Motor Vehicle Production in the United States

Year	Passenger Cars	Trucks and Buses	Total
1900	4,192	—	4,192
1905	24,250	750	25,000
1910	181,000	6,000	187,000
1915	895,930	74,000	969,930
1920	1,905,560	321,789	2,227,349
1925	3,735,171	530,659	4,265,830

Tons of Waste

The twentieth century suffered recessions and a major economic depression, but overall the economies of developed nations boomed. More natural resources were cut down, mined, processed, and made into consumer goods then ever before in human history. What did this burst of human activity mean to the planet's environment? It meant more depletion of natural resources, more pollution of the soil, water, and air, and an explosion of waste.

WORKERS IN GUIYU, CHINA, SORTING THROUGH SOME OF THE MILLIONS OF COMPUTERS AND OTHER ELECTRONIC DEVICES DISCARDED BY DEVELOPED COUNTRIES.

One law of a consumer society is, the more we produce, the more we waste. This waste comes at both ends of the production-consumption cycle. First we'll look at the production end. In the rush to turn out as much product in order to make as much profit as possible, manufacturers use resources at alarming rates. The amount of material needed to make a single semiconductor chip is over 100,000 times the weight of the actual chip. For a laptop computer, it's close to four thousand times. To produce a quart of orange juice it takes a thousand quarts of water and two quarts of gasoline. A ton of paper takes 98 tons of water, trees, and other resources. It takes 1,000 tons of freshwater to grow a ton of wheat.

Then, of course, once the product is made, the waste that's not recycled or properly disposed of turns into pollution. This can lead to an environmental catastrophe.

Minamata and Mercury

The Minamata, Japan, catastrophe took place over many agonizing years, building to a deadly climax. The town was tiny when a chemical factory opened in 1910. By 1950 the population had grown to 50,000. Many of the townspeople worked in the chemical factory and depended on it for their livelihood.

The factory turned out petrochemicals and plastics. The town of Minamata faces the Shiranui Sea, and Minamata Bay is part of that sea. Between 1932 and 1968, the factory dumped an estimated 27 tons of mercury compounds into the Minamata Bay. When mercury meets water, it gets converted into methylmercury, a toxic organic compound that has this in common with DDT: it works its way up the food chain. This toxic form of mercury accumulated in the tissues of the fish of Minamata Bay, which

SOME OF THE THOUSANDS OF VICTIMS OF THE POISONING
OF MINAMATA BAY

the people of Minamata relied on for their chief source of protein. The more fish they ate, the more toxic methylmercury accumulated in their tissues.

The effects of mercury poisoning showed up first in fish and cats. During the 1940s, fish in the bay began dying in great numbers. Then, in the 1950s, the cats of Minamata began acting more than a little strangely. At first they would stagger around as if drunk. Then they would jerk and skitter as if dancing some demonic dance, then vomit, and then die. People called this escalating parade of toxic symptoms the cat-dancing disease.

In the mid–1950s, it struck the children. Methylmercury attacks the central nervous system. Children had trouble hearing; they heard ringing in their ears. Then they started feeling tired and numb. They had trouble keeping their balance. The methylmercury was damaging their brains. They were suffering from what people now called "Minamata Disease."

Minamata Bay once supported a strong local fishing industry, but no one would buy the catch anymore. Still, the factory kept dumping mercury into the bay as thousands of people fell sick from eating contaminated fish. For years people feared that the mercury from the factory was the cause of it all. Why hadn't they voiced their fears? The factory was the town's chief employer. Without it, many families would be left without work. The Minamata tragedy showed how economic needs can overrule even deadly serious environmental and health concerns.

Finally, people did take action and sued the factory. In 1973, the factory lost in court. By then more than 1,400 people had died of Minamata Disease. The court ordered factory owners to pay the victims and their families around $100 million in damages. Later, government workers dredged Minamata Bay and decontaminated it at a cost of $500 million. Today, Minamata Bay is safe to fish in once again.

PCBs and Anniston

The United States has had its share of towns poisoned by waste from factories and mines. One of the worst was Anniston, Alabama. The chief poison was a combination of chemicals known as PCBs, used in the manufacture of electrical equipment. The Monsanto Corporation manufactured PCBs in Anniston for forty years.

In 1977 the federal government banned PCBs. By that time Monsanto had dumped a reported 10 million pounds of PCB waste into landfills and 1.2 million pounds into streams. Anniston also received widespread doses of lead poisoning from an iron mining operation. The mine sold the dirt dug up as fill for construction projects, spreading the lead-contaminated dirt all over town.

Meanwhile, an abnormally high number of Anniston residents developed kidney and liver problems and contracted cancer. The area led the state in the number of birth defects to newborn children. Anniston became known as Toxic Town.

Some 3,600 Anniston residents joined together to file a class action lawsuit against Monsanto, similar to the one filed by the Minamata victims. The court ruling was the same. In February 2002, Monsanto was found liable for damage caused by polluting the area's soil and water and poisoning residents with PCBs. As of 2004, courts were still trying to determine how much money Monsanto owed the Anniston residents poisoned by PCBs.

Less or More?

During the trial, company documents were presented as evidence showing Monsanto knew that PCBs were toxic to animals—which meant they could easily be harmful to humans. They knew this as far back as 1938. Yet Monsanto kept these facts secret and continued dumping PCBs, just as the Minamata factory owners kept dumping mercury. Environmentalists point to cases like these as proof that industry still practices frontier economics, even when harming the environment means harming human beings.

But what about the fact that individual factories have been cutting down on pollution? Each year U.S. industries release smaller amounts of pollutants for each unit of goods produced. There are several reasons why. Engineers have developed packaging systems that use less material, such as lightweight plastic instead of heavy glass bottles. They have also developed smaller and more compact products.

A computer in the 1950s, for example, was the size and weight of a small house and could process only about a thousand instructions per second. A laptop computer today is the size of a magazine and can easily process more than a billion instructions per second. Manufacturers call this process "dematerialization." They also have developed more efficient ways of sending information. In years past, documents had to be sent by mail in trucks, planes, and boats that guzzled fossil fuels. Today they can be sent almost anywhere in the world in a matter of seconds electronically at far less harm to the environment.

Environmentalists do not dispute these positive trends. What they do dispute is how we should interpret them. They are not signs that industry is doing less harm to the environment, they say. In fact, the opposite is true. As we create products that use less material per unit, we also produce more and more units that are bought by more and more people. As the population grows, so does the total number of factories, the total amount of goods produced, and the total amount of pollution and waste left behind.

Waste not Wasted

One way to reduce this waste is to recycle it—collect and reuse it. Sanitation workers in New York and Boston developed a new slang term, "mongo." It means garbage that gets picked up and reused, often for a different purpose. The practice has existed throughout human history. Today it's most common in poor countries, where people don't have the money to buy or build a conventional dwelling and must concoct one from whatever stray scraps of wood, tin, rock, and cardboard they can lay their hands on. Shantytowns housing millions of people in developing countries such as South Africa, Thailand, and Mexico are built mostly from mongo.

In the United States mongo shows up in homes as well, in the form of straw. Most grain growers burn the stubble left in their fields after they finish harvesting. But burning pollutes the air, so some growers have been baling the stubble and treating it as mongo instead. They sell it to builders, who wire-stitch the bales together to make walls, then stucco them on the outside and plaster them on the inside. A home insulated with straw bales is warmer in winter and cooler in summer. It's also quiet. The straw smothers the noisy sounds of traffic and loud neighbors. These straw-insulated homes are good examples of what environmentalists call a "green building" approach to housing.

Green Building

Some architects, contractors, business owners, and homeowners look at the structures they create and own from a sustainable-living point of view.

Green buildings are energy efficient. For example, factories are built with more glass to let in more natural light and reduce the amount of electricity used. Green builders, trained in energy-efficient construction, install heating and cooling systems that are "tuned" to the local climate and use less energy. Homeowners insulate their attics and put weather stripping around doors to cut down on heating costs.

Green buildings are also resource efficient because builders use construction materials, such as mineral fiber insulation and structural wood products, made from recycled materials in construction. When planning plumbing, they are careful to use the shortest possible length of pipe to hook up each faucet to the water heater. Homeowners install low-flush toilets, low-flow shower heads and faucets, and dishwashers and washing machines with water-miser features.

Mongo Fish and Worms

Fish can become mongo as well. Leo Ray runs a super-efficient fish farming business along the Snake River in Idaho. He taps into geothermal springs for free warm water to house his catfish, trout, tilapia, and sturgeon. It's a big operation and, inevitably, some of the fish die before Ray can harvest them to sell.

What to do with these dead fish? Ray looked at them as mongo—and saw alligators. He bought some in Florida to raise on his Idaho farm, and fed them the dead fish. So the alligators became an efficient, low-cost fish disposal system. Later, when the gators are full grown, Ray makes a profit by selling them for meat and hides.

Then there are the food scraps from Wright-Patterson Air Force Base in Ohio. The base's mess hall feeds many soldiers and leaves much waste. Each day's 500-pounds-worth of spoiled fruit and vegetable trimmings used to be hauled away to landfills. Then Bill Meinderding, who managed the base's recycling program, got the bright idea of feeding them to worms instead.

Thousands of worms were put into flat dirt beds in a dark building on the base. Each day's scraps were layered on top, and the worms went right to work. In three weeks they had processed seven tons of scraps. The worm farm saved the air force base the cost of having the scraps hauled away—and more. The worm waste, called castings, was collected and used on lawns around the base instead of chemical fertilizers. The organic castings, besides being free, reduced harmful fertilizer runoff into neighboring streams and groundwater.

Mongo and Composting

We all have our share of mongo. Every day we throw away things that could be useful if we looked at them from a sustainable-living mindset. Vegetable peelings, coffee grounds, leaves, and other organic wastes can be turned into what gardeners refer to as black gold, or compost.

Lots of people compost in their backyards. The process is based on an elementary scientific principle. Organic wastes get broken down through natural chemical and biological processes. Worms, insects, bacteria, and other microorganisms do most of the chewing up and breaking down. The rest is done by exposure to air and water. The result is thick, rich dirt ideal for growing things.

A simple container is all you need. This can be bought at a hardware store or built by hand. A metal barrel or garbage can with holes punched in the side and the bottom removed will do. Your compost pile consists of layers of organic mongo alternated with layers of dirt. Each layer should be about 2 inches (5 cm) thick. Every now and then stick a pitchfork or shovel down into it and turn and mix it so everything eventually gets exposed to the open air.

Environmentalists look at composting this way: Now, instead of contributing to the glut of garbage in landfills, compost turns some of your waste into black gold. Every day all around the world tons of topsoil is lost to wind and water erosion. Composting adds a little of this valuable resource back into Spaceship Earth.

Waterlogged Logs and Cow Dung

When Scott Mitchen looked down at the logs at the bottom of Lake Superior, he saw mongo. During the 1800s, lumberjacks cut down millions of trees and floated them across the lake, from Ontario, Canada, to Michigan. About one of every ten sank during the trip. These were not ordinary trees. Some dated from the 1500s. They were stronger and denser than ordinary trees. Their fine-grained wood was highly prized by architects and builders. So Mitchen hired teams of divers to raise the waterlogged logs. It was not easy. Some weighed as much as 5,000 pounds. But Mitchen's mongo-inspired plan turned into profits.

So did a plan by a group of British dairy farmers. They decided that dung from their five thousand cows could be turned into power. So they built a biogas plant on the north coast of Devon, England, and had the cow dung collected and stored. As it fermented, it produced methane gas, which was collected for use in gas-fired generators. The plant's generators produced enough electricity to power nine hundred homes.

Dirty Work

These mongo-inspired strategies are at work around the world, in poor and rich nations alike. More people are beginning to see the mountains of waste we humans produce as potential wealth.

Guiyu, China, is one of those places. China desperately needs jobs, and the United States needs someplace safe to dump its millions of used-up computers, printers, and other electronic equipment. In 2001 alone, Americans discarded more than 40 million computers. Personal computers and printers look harmless, but inside are toxic wastes that can't be dumped into landfills. People somewhere must do the dirty work of taking them apart, recycling the usable parts, and disposing of the toxic elements.

Those people are the residents of Guiyu. About 80 percent of discarded U.S. computers are loaded onto ships and sent there. Breaking them down, separating out the reusable parts, and disposing of toxic elements is done there for about one-tenth of what it would cost if U.S. workers did the job. Wages in China are low by U.S. standards, but the people of Guiyu need the work, which will increase in years to come as U.S. computer sales keep rising.

The health of the workers and their environment suffers, though. The streets of Guiyu are heaped with mounds of old computers. Workers haul them into sheds and break them apart with their hands. This can be extremely unhealthy work. Workers inhale black clouds of lead toner when they handle computer printers. The Lianjiang River runs through town, but drinking water must be brought in from miles away because the waters of the Lianjiang are black with lead and other metals that workers dump there. The World Health Organization declared the Lianjiang's water unsafe after tests showed it contained 190 times the amount of lead that was safe for humans to drink.

The Shipbreakers

China gets most of the developed world's computers to break up. India, Pakistan, and Bangladesh get most of the undeveloped world's cargo ships. Alang, in southern India, is a town built entirely on the industry of breaking up the world's big ships when they get too old and expensive to run. These are the world's biggest ships, tankers and supertankers like the *Prestige* and the *Exxon Valdez*, weighing tens of thousands of tons. About half of them eventually end up on Alang's six-mile (9.6 km) stretch of oily, greasy sand. The huge tides there make conditions right for beaching the massive vessels at high tide and tying them down along the long, flat beach. Then men from Alang's work force of 40,000 swarm over them, cutting them apart for scrap metal.

The work in Alang is far dirtier and more dangerous than the work in Guiyu. The shipbreakers are exposed to fires, explosions, falls from hundreds of feet, and poisons from fuel oil, lubricants, insulation, wiring, paint, and the toxic slop left in cargo holds. There are injuries every day, and each year workers die. In 1997 at least fifteen men were killed when sparks from a cutting torch set off an explosion of gases in a ship's hold.

The metal cut from one supertanker may bring as much as $1 million on the international scrap market. But little of this profit ends up in workers' pockets. They are paid low wages and live in a nearby shantytown in shacks built of bits and pieces of the broken ships, alongside a marsh infested with malaria-carrying mosquitoes. But in India's poor economy, a shipbreaking job means a living wage these men might not find anyplace else.

Good Intentions

Greenpeace is an international organization dedicated to stopping environmental harm. Its members, most of whom live in rich nations, want to improve the living conditions of people in poor nations. Greenpeace has taken up the cause of the Alang shipbreakers, and has launched a campaign to secure them safer working conditions and better housing. Greenpeace also wants governments to stop the shipbreaking industry from polluting the beaches and waters of Alang and other shipbreaking sites in poor nations.

Greenpeace has good intentions, but the shipbreakers do not welcome them. Pravin S. Nagarsheth is president of the Indian Shipbreakers Association in Mumbai. He sums up their objections this way:

The fact remains that workers at Alang are better paid and are probably safer than their counterparts back in the poor

> **provinces. . . . To provide housing and better
> living conditions . . . is financially impractical
> for a developing country like India, where
> forty-five percent of the population is living
> below the poverty line.**

A reporter who interviewed Alang shipbreakers quoted one worker as saying, "The question I want to ask the environmentalists is if you should want to die first of starvation or pollution."

Warming the Globe

We have looked at how human activities transform different parts of the planet. Now let's look at the planet as a whole. Earth's overall temperature is slowly rising, and the chief reason is the carbon dioxide (CO_2) that all the world's nations release into the air when burning fossil fuels. This temperature rise is known as global warming, or global climate change.

Global warming changed our view of CO_2. We once saw it as purely a good and natural thing. After all, carbon dioxide is the gas that humans and animals exhale and that plants must absorb to live and grow. Now, thanks to human activities, many people see the growing amounts of CO_2 in the air as too much of a good thing, upsetting the balance of nature and throwing the biosphere out of balance.

There are two big reasons for the rise in atmospheric CO_2, and both are economic. First, as world populations and economies grow, people buy more cars and use more electric power, and automobiles and coal-fired power

AERIAL PHOTOS OF THE ANTARCTIC APPEAR TO SHOW THE EFFECTS OF GLOBAL WARMING.

plants are the chief CO_2 polluters. And second, growing economies also demand more wood. Since the 1960s we have cut down huge chunks of the world's forests without replacing them, including 15 percent of the Amazon rain forests. Scientists call forests "carbon sinks" because they absorb CO_2. When we cut forests down, less CO_2 gets absorbed, and more remains in the atmosphere to warm the planet.

The Greenhouse Effect

How does CO_2 raise Earth's temperature? Carbon dioxide is called a greenhouse gas because it acts like the glass in greenhouse windows. A portion of the sunlight that strikes

Earth is reflected back into outer space. But greenhouse gases deflect some of it back to further heat up the planet. Scientists call this the Greenhouse Effect.

Methane (CH_4) is the other chief greenhouse gas in the atmosphere. We add to its volume in several ways. We raise millions of head of cattle that release tons of CH_4 by enteric generation, also known as "passing gas." We release it by methanogenesis when we flood soil to grow rice. As the garbage we dump into landfills breaks down, it releases CH_4 in a process called anaerobic fermentation. We also release methane gas when we drill and mine for fossil fuels.

Hundreds of scientists from around the world have studied the possible effects of greenhouse gases on Earth's future climate. Their predictions were released in a 2003 report by the Intergovernmental Panel on Climate Change (IPCC) of the United Nations. During this century, greenhouse gases could warm the planet's surface temperature by anywhere from 2.5 to 10.4 degrees Fahrenheit (1.4 to 5.8 degrees Celsius), the report said.

Suppose these scientists turn out to be right. What then? Reactions were mixed. Some experts said not to worry. Places with cold climates, such as the northern United States and Canada, would get a little warmer, and places with warm climates would see little temperature change. Meanwhile, the increase in CO_2 would make plants everywhere grow thicker and taller. In other words, raising Earth's temperature would be a good thing.

Others saw a lot to worry about. They predicted an increase in extreme weather events, such as hurricanes, tornadoes, drought, and torrential rains that lead to flooding. They said the polar ice caps might melt, which would make sea levels rise, which would flood coastlines everywhere and put some island nations entirely underwater. In the worst case scenario, the ocean currents that carry warm water toward the poles would shut down, plunging the planet into the frigid depths of a new ice age.

Emissions Trading

Climate experts disagree on what may happen, but most of them do agree that global climate change is for real. As long as populations and economies keep growing, Earth's environment will keep heating up. A 2003 *Washington Post* editorial said, "Recent studies on everything from changing wildlife behavior patterns to the condition of polar ice shelves all indicate that the Earth is growing warmer. . . . [F]ew now dispute the increased presence of greenhouse gases in the atmosphere or question the role that human activity, since the Industrial Revolution, has played in creating them."

Even the companies that produce fossil fuels admit that their products are raising Earth's temperature. One of the biggest is ChevronTexaco. In an official statement the company said, "One of the environmental concerns we all share is global climate change. We recognize that the use of fossil fuels has contributed to an increase in greenhouse gases—mainly carbon dioxide and methane—in the earth's atmosphere."

Some energy companies have taken steps to counter global climate change. One is British oil giant BP, which helps fund research to develop the renewable sources of solar energy and fuel-cell technologies. BP also designed a company-wide plan to reduce its own CO_2 emissions. The plan is based on emissions trading. BP has 150 business units scattered over more than one hundred countries. Each unit uses fossil fuels and emits greenhouse gases in its daily operations. BP set up an emissions limit for each unit, a target, and encouraged units to trade with one another. If a unit reduced its greenhouse gas emissions beyond the target limit, it could sell its extra credits to units that needed them to meet their limits. Units also got extra credit for using less fuel in their daily operations.

Business units that reduced their emissions and cut fuel

use received higher pay and bonuses. In 2001, BP chief executive Lord John Browne announced the results for the plan's first year of operation. BP business units not only met their targets, but went beyond them. The plan helped BP's profits as well as the environment, Lord Browne announced. While the 150 business units reduced their emissions and fuel consumption, they also saved $600 million in the process.

Resistance

U.S. president George W. Bush has a free-market attitude toward emissions reductions. He favors voluntary plans like BP's and opposed mandatory regulations, where companies had to reduce emissions by certain amounts set by the government or face fines. Bush has said that government regulation of CO_2 emissions "does not make economic sense for America."

Few U.S. businesses are following BP's example, and the United States continues to lead the world in greenhouse gas emissions. Americans generated some 45,000 pounds of CO_2 per person per year, twice as much as the average Japanese or European and many times more than a citizen of a poor nation. Political commentator David Brooks has called the Bush administration's response to global warming "a pitiable voluntary program, which has had no effect."

Meanwhile, the economies of poor nations, such as China and India, are predicted to boom. This means their people will buy more vehicles and use more power. These nations cannot afford to use the more expensive technologies that rich nations use to produce energy at relatively low pollution levels. Instead, they will have to turn to the old, inefficient fossil fuel-burning technologies that rich nations used in the past. And that means the enormous volumes of additional greenhouse gases they generate will further warm the global climate.

Rich nations do not want poor nations to do as they did, but poor nations say they have no choice. After talking to workers on a visit to especially poor areas of India, one reporter wrote in *Atlantic* magazine that "Resentful Indians kept saying to me, 'You had your industrial revolution, and so we should have ours.'"

Conclusion

Now what? Where is all this global depletion of resources and pollution of the biosphere leading us? The average North American uses about seven times the resources of the average Asian or African consumer. As the economies of China, India, and other developing nations gear up, so will the consumption of natural resources. Suppose their standards of living continue to rise, as experts predict? Can everyone on Earth eventually enjoy the standard of living of the richest nations?

The most comprehensive information we have to answer this question comes from large-scale research studies such as *Living Planet Report* (LPR), released in 2002 by the World Wildife Fund. The LPR examines the ecological footprint (EF). The EF measures humanity's consumption of renewable resources: forests, freshwater, marine life, and arable land. Between 1961 and 1999, the EF grew by 80 percent, which put it well beyond the Earth's sustainable capacity. And the EF rises each year. Think of withdrawing more money from a bank account each day and putting nothing back in. Day by day humanity's supply of natural resources falls lower and lower.

This was not a problem for early humans who enjoyed a vast bounty of natural resources to support their tiny, scattered populations. They didn't have to worry about depleting the planet's resources or polluting its environment. They could afford to live by a frontier-economics mind set.

Today more than 6 billion humans walk the Earth, and more are added each day. This book has shown how the ecological footprint has grown to its present point. Are we now coming to the point where the natural world no longer holds enough fossil fuels or freshwater or forests or marine life or fertile soil to satisfy humanity's needs and wants? According to the LPR, "[I]t is very unlikely that the Earth would be able to run an ecological overdraft for another 50 years without some severe ecological backlashes undermining future population and economic growth."

Other experts think we might have until the end of the century, perhaps longer, before vital resources start hitting serious limits. Most experts tend to agree on one thing, though: We have so much to learn about the mysterious workings of nature that we may never know exactly where we stand. Environmental historian John McNeill put it this way:

> **It is impossible to know whether humankind has entered a genuine ecological crisis. It is clear enough that our current ways are ecologically unsustainable, but we cannot know for how long we may yet sustain them, or what might happen if we do.**

Some say this uncertainty means we should take a wait-and-see approach. This applies to global climate change as well as resource depletion. President George W.

Bush said we should not take strict, all-out measures to reduce greenhouse gases. These strict measures would slow the economy, he said, and we still can't be certain that global warming really will have serious consequences in the future.

Others say we can't afford to wait, that human beings and the natural world may be on a collision course. As the LPR says, "[I]t would be far better to control our own destiny than to leave it to nature."

We can start gaining control only by reducing humanity's ecological footprint. This book has shown strategies and technologies that agents of change use to help, such as drip irrigation, marine sanctuaries, hybrid cars, and solar-energy units. They have some things in common. They mean setting aside the frontier-economics attitude that sees the natural world as limitless and invulnerable. They mean taking up a sustainable-living viewpoint that sees resources as limited and fragile. They mean lowering our short-term expectations for the long-term good of all life on Earth. The authors of *Limits To Growth*, another large-scale research study, summed thing up this way:

> **There is no possibility of raising material consumption levels for everyone to the levels now enjoyed by the rich. Everyone should have their fundamental material needs satisfied. Material needs beyond this level should be satisfied only if it is possible, for all, within a sustainable ecological footprint.**

Notes

Chapter 1

p. 11, "Gold Rush Overview," California State Parks, May 6, 2004, www.parks.ca.gov/default.asp?page_id=1081. (Accessed July 10, 2003.)

p. 13, Twain, Mark. *Roughing It,* vol. 1. New York: Harper & Row, 1899, pp. 186 and 244.

p. 15, "New Perspectives on the West." PBS. www.pbs.org/weta/thewest/events/1890_1900.htm (Accessed August 10, 2004.)

p. 15, McNeill, J. R. *Something New Under the Sun: An Environmental History of the Twentieth-Century World.* New York: W. W. Norton & Company, 2000, p. 357.

Chapter Two

p. 16, Carson, Rachel. *Silent Spring.* Boston: Houghton Mifflin Company, 1962, p. 15.

p. 20, "Environmental Movement Timeline," EcoTopiaUSA, June 17, 2003, www.ectopia.org/ehof/timeline.html (Accessed July 10, 2003.)

Chapter Three

p. 26, Rothenberg, Jennie. "In Defense of the Forests," *The Atlantic* online. December 18, 2002, www.theatlantic.com/unbound/flashbks/muirforests.htm (Accessed July 7, 2003.)

p. 26, Rothenberg.

p. 28, "Progress Report on Implementing President Bush's Healthy Forests Initiative." United States Department of Agriculture, www.healthyforests.gov/learn_more/index.html (Accessed February 23, 2004.)

p. 28, Progress Report.

p. 30, "Ecology Hall of Fame: Julia 'Butterfly' Hill," EcoTopiaUSA. www.ecotopia.org/ehof/hill/bio.html (Accessed June 8, 2004.)

p. 31, "Federally Sanctioned Mining Abuses Even Worse Under Bush Rule Changes." *Greenwatch Today*, May 13, 2004 www.bushgreenwatch.org/print/index.ph (Accessed June 10, 2003.)

p. 32, "Conservation Groups Respond to BLM Oil & Gas Lease Withdrawals," The Wilderness Society. May 13, 2004, www.wilderness.org/NewsRoom/release/20040513b.cfm. (Accessed June 10, 2003.)

p. 32, "Historical National Population Estimates." U.S. Census Bureau www.census.gov/population/estimates/nation/ popclockest.txt (Accessed June 14, 2004.)

p. 32, "Population Clock." U.S. Census Bureau, www.census.gov/main/www/popclock.html (Accessed June 14, 2004.)

p. 33, Johnson, Kirk. "Counting the Costs of Growth With a Forest of Formulas," *New York Times*, November 23, 2003, www.nytimes.com/2003/11/23/weekinreview/23JOHN.htm. (Accessed Dec. 7, 2003.)

p. 34, "The Endangered Species Act of 1973, Findings, Purposes, and Policy," U.S. Fish and Wildlife Service, http://endangered.fws.gov/esa.html#Lnk020 (Accessed August 11, 2004.)

p. 35, "Endangered Fly Stalls Some California Projects," *New York Times*, December 1, 2002, www.nytimes.com/2002/12/01/national/01FLY.html (Accessed Jan. 5, 2003.)

p. 35, Jacobs, Andrew. "New Jersey Governor Enlists Himself in 'War on Sprawl,'" *New York Times*, January 2, 2003 www.nytimes.com/2003/01/02/nyregion/02MCGR.html (Accessed Jan. 5, 2003.)

p. 36, Ritter, John. "Calif. Housing Battle Creates an Odd Alliance," *USA Today*, Sept. 12, 2002, www.usatoday.com/news/nation/2002-12-09-sierra-usat_x.htm (Accessed Oct. 10, 2002).

p. 36, Braun, Richard. "Nature's Affirmative Action," *Tech Central Station*, November 13, 2003, www2.techcentral station.com/1051/printer.jsp?CID=1051-111303D (Accessed Dec. 7, 2003.)

p. 37, Stuart, Virginia. "The Species Race," *University of New Hampshire* magazine, Fall 2003, p. 28.

p. 40, "About Us." Seacology, www.seacology.org/about/index.html (Accessed February 28, 2003.)

Chapter Four

p. 45, "Into the Dead Zone: Galveston Researcher Examines Loss of Marine Life," *Science Daily*, May 6, 2004, www.sciencedaily.com/print.php?url=/ releases/2004/05/040507082408.htm. (Accessed June 10, 2004.)

p. 45, "150 'dead zones' counted in oceans,' MSNBC, March 29, 2004, www.msnbc.msn.com/id/4624359. (Accessed May 7, 2004.)

p. 47, "The Transformation of Animals Into Food: Environmental Destruction." *Vegan Outreach*, www.veganoutreach.org/whyvegan/environment.html (Accessed February 3, 2004.)

p. 47, "The Transformation."

p. 48, Carlton, Jim. "Green Group Tries To Drive Ranchers Off Federal Lands," *Wall Street Journal*, November 11, 2002, pp. A1 and A9.

p. 49, "Grazed to the Bone: Public Lands Ranching in the West," Forest Guardians, www.fguardians.org/grazingreform.htm (Accessed July 7, 2004.)

p. 49, Carlton.

p. 49, Carlton.

Chapter Five

p. 50, Weiss, Rick. "Water Scarcity Prompts Scientists to Look Down," *Washington Post*, March 10, 2003, p. A11.

p. 50, McNeill, p. 121.

p. 51, Meadows, Donella, Jorgen Randers, and Dennis Meadows. *Limits to Growth*, White River Junction, VT: Chelsea Green Publishing Company, 2004, p. 71.

p. 51, "Ogallala Aquifer."
www.npwd.org/Ogallala.htm (Accessed Jan. 9, 2003.)

p. 51, Dowie, Mark. "In Law We Trust," *Orion*, July/August
2003. www.oriononline.org/pages/om/03-4om/Dowie.html.
(Accessed Sept. 10, 2003.)

p. 52, Dowie.

p. 53, McNeill, p. 189.

p. 53, "Bush Marks Earth Day, Talks of 'Progress,'" *New York
Times*, April 22, 2004,
www.nytimes.com/aponline/national/AP-Bush.html

p. 54, Sanger, David and David Halbfinger. "For Earth Day, Bush
and Kerry Vie on Environment," *New York Times*,
April 23, 2004,
www.nytimes.com/2004/04/23/politics/campaign/23BUSH.html.
(Accessed May 3, 2004.)

p. 55, Barringer, Felicity. "Michigan Landowner Who Filled
Wetlands Faces Prison." *New York Times*, May 18, 2004,
www.nytimes.com/2004/05/18/national/18enviro.html
(Accessed June 10, 2004.)

p. 57, "Mansfield Developer Arraigned On Charges He
Destroyed Mansfield Wetlands," Office of Massachusetts
Attorney General,
www.ago.state.ma.us/sp.cfm?pageid=986&id=1167
(Accessed January 22, 2004.)

p. 61, Pala, Christopher. "$85 Million Project Begins for Revival
of the Aral Sea," Jan. 22, 2004, *New York Times*, August
5, 2003.www.nytimes.com/2003/08/05/science/earth/05ARAL.html.
(Accessed Feb. 10, 2004.)

p. 63, Smith, Craig S. "Saudis Worry as They Waste Their Scarce
Water," *New York Times*, January 26, 2003,
www.nytimes.com/2003/01/26/international/middleeast/26SAUD.html
(Accessed Feb. 10, 2004.)

p. 63, Rauch, Jonathan. "Will Frankenfood Save the Planet?"
The Atlantic online, October 2003,
www.theatlantic.com/cgi-bin/send.cgi?page=http%3A//
www.theatlantic.com/issues/2003/10/rauch.htm.
(Accessed Nov. 17, 2004.)

p. 63, Taylor, James. M. "Researchers Announce Breakthrough
on Salt-Tolerant Crops," *Environment News*, October 1, 2001,
www.heartland.org/Article.cfm?artID=857
(Accessed Dec. 10, 2004.)

p. 66, McNeill, p. 146.

p. 66, "Prestige Oil Spill Far Worse Than Thought," *NewScientist.com*, August 27, 2003, www.newscientist.com/news/news.jsp?id=ns99994100 (Accessed Sept. 10, 2003.)

p. 68, Simons, Marlise. "France Clamps Down on Shipping Pollution," *New York Times*, April 7, 2003, www.nytimes.com/2003/04/07/international/europe/07FRAN.html (Accessed May 5, 2003.)

p. 69, Lazaroff, Cat. "Ocean Crisis Caused by Destructive Fishing," *Environment News Service*, February 19, 2003, ensj-news.com/ens/feb2003/2003-02-18-06.asp. (Accessed March 5, 2003.)

p. 69, "Millennium Development Goals: A Compact Among Nations to End Human Poverty, Overview." United Nations Human Development, 2003, p. 10, www.undp.org/hdr2003 (Accessed Feb. 1, 2004.)

p. 71, Lazaroff.

p. 71, Clarke, Thurston. "'The Empty Ocean': Invisible Extinctions," *New York Times*, May 25, 2003, www.nytimes.com/2003/05/25/books/review/25CLARKET.html (Accessed June 6, 2003.)

p. 71, Lazaroff.

p. 72, Walton, Marsha. "Report: Caribbean coral reefs down 80 percent." CNN, July 17, 2003, www.cnn.com/2003/TECH/science/07/17/cooisc.coral/index.html (Accessed Aug. 8, 2003.)

p. 73, Lazaroff.

p. 73, "The Promise of a Blue Revolution," *The Economist*, August 7, 2003. www.economist.com/business/displayStory.cfm?story_id=1974103 (Accessed Aug. 15, 2003.)

p. 74, Pinsky, Malin, and Kristin Hunter-Thomson. "Agriculture v. Aquaculture in Patagonia," *Tidepool*, May 20, 2004, www.tidepool.org/original_content.cfm?articleid=117266 (Accessed June 6, 2004.)

p. 74, Clarke.

p. 74, Pinsky.

p. 75, "The Promise."

Chapter Six
p. 77, McNeill, p. 15.

p. 79, "Industry Statistics: Petroleum Facts At a Glance: July 2004," American Petroleum Institute. api-ec.api.org/industry/index.cfm?objectid=DAC33528-7704-11D5-BC6A00B0D0E15BFC&method=display_body&er=1&bitmask=001004000000000000 (Accessed Aug. 12, 2004.)

p. 80, "Oil Imports Reach 64.5%." ANWR, July 12, 2004, www.anwr.org/archives/oil_imports_reach_645.php#more (Accessed Aug. 12, 2004.)

p. 80, Burnett, H. Sterling. "The Drive for Solutions; Drilling Would Ease U.S. Dependence," National Center for Policy Analysis. May 23, 2004. www.ncpa.org/abo/cd/052304drive.htm (Accessed Aug. 12, 2004.)

p. 80, "Drilling in ANWR: An Empty Promise for U.S. Energy Policy," Democratic Policy Committee, democrats.senate.gov/~dpc/pubs/107-1-72.html (Accessed July 15, 2004.)

p. 81, Pegg, J. R. "North Slope Report Fuels Alaska Drilling Debate," *Environment News Service*, March 5, 2003, http://ens-news.com/ens/mar2003/2003-03-05-10.asp (Accessed June 6, 2003.)

p. 81, "AlaskaWild Update #215: Senate and House Budget Committees Both Drop Arctic Drilling Proposal From Budget." Alaska Wilderness League, March 12, 2004, www.alaskawild.org/takeaction_alaskawild_update.html (Accessed May 10, 2004.)

p. 84, "Green Autos in the Showroom, But Few on the Road," *Environment News Service*, February 21, 2003, http://ens-news.com/ens/feb2003/2003-02-21-11.asp (Accessed June 6, 2004.)

p. 84, Hakim, Danny. "Average U.S. Car Is Tipping Scales at 4,000 Pounds," *New York Times*, May 5, 2004, www.nytimes.com/2004/05/05/business/05weight.html (Accessed May 10, 2004.)

p. 84, Bowers, Andy. "California's SUV Ban," *Slate*, August 4, 2004, www.slate.msn.com/id/2104755 (Accessed Sept. 10, 2004.)

p. 85, Hakim, Danny. "Safety Gap Grows Wider Between S.U.V.'s and Cars," *New York Times*, August 17, 2004, www.nytimes.com/2004/08/17/business/17auto.html?hp (Accessed Sept. 10, 2004.)

p. 85, "Guzzling Gas," *Washington Post*, March 29, 2004, p. A22.

p. 86, Shirouzu, Norihiko and Jeffrey Ball. "Revolution Under the Hood," *Wall Street Journal*, May 12, 2004, p. B–1.

p. 87, Hakim, Danny. "Hybrid Cars Are Catching On," *New York Times*, January 28, 2003, www.nytimes.com/2003/01/28/business/28HYBR.html (Accessed Feb. 3, 2003)

p. 87, Shirouzu.

pp. 89–90, "Senator Edwards Works To Block Bush Administration Backsliding on Clean Air," News From Senator John Edwards, January 16, 2003, www.senate.gov/~edwards/press/2003/0116-pr.html (Accessed Feb. 8, 2003.)

p. 90, Lee, Jennifer. "Clear Skies No More for Millions as Pollution Rule Expands," *New York Times*, April 13, 2004, www.nytimes.com/2004/04/13/national/13AIR.html (Accessed May 10, 2004.)

p. 91, Lee.

p. 91, "Governor Rendell Unveils 2004–05 Budget," StatePulse.com, February 2, 2004, www.statepulse.com/Pennsylvania/2004/02.04.04.gov.pr.asp (Accessed May 10, 2004.)

p. 92, McNeill, p. 150.

p. 92, McNeill, p. 159.

p. 92, "Wonders of the World Databank: Three Gorges Dam," Building Big, www.pbs.org/wgbh/buidlingbig/wonder/structure/three_gorges.html (Accessed July 19, 2004.)

p. 92, "Wonders."

p. 95, "Chernobyl Nuclear Disaster," www.chernobyl.co.uk/homef.html (Accessed July 20, 2004.)

p. 95, McNeill, p. 312.

p. 96, McNeill, p. 313.

p. 96, Wald, Matthew L. "Hopes of Building Nation's First New Nuclear Plant in Decades," *New York Times*, March 31, 2004, www.nytimes.com/2004/03/31/politics/31NUKE.html (Accessed May 10, 2004.)

p. 96, "Radioactive Waste Disposal: An Environmental Perspective," U.S. Environmental Protection Agency, www.epa.gov/radiation/docs/radwaste (Accessed July 20, 2004.)

p. 97, Jacobs, Andrew. "South Carolina Town Welcomes Nuclear Waste," *International Herald Tribune*, March 30, 2004, www.iht.com/articles/512519.htm (Accessed April 6, 2004.)

p. 98, "UNEP Ties Up with Homes to Boost Solar Home Systems," Business Line Internet Edition, March 7, 2003, www.blonnet.com/2003/03/08/stories/2003030800520400.htm (Accessed March 10, 2003.)

Chapter Seven
p. 101, McNeill, p. 315.

p. 102, www.thehenryford.org/education/smartfun/modelt/ carowners/autoprod.html (Accessed Nov. 30, 2003)

p. 104, McKusker, John J. "Comparing the Purchasing Power of Money in the United States (or Colonies) from 1665 to 2003," Economic History Services, 2004, www.eh.net/hmit/ppowerusd/ (Accessed Sept. 12, 2004.)

p. 104, Hawken, Paul, Amory Lovins, and L. Hunter Lovins. *Natural Capitalism: Creating the Next Industrial Revolution.* New York: Little, Brown and Company, 1999, p. 50.

p. 106, Meadows, p. 72.

p. 107, Kirby, Alex. "UN Urges 'Drastic' Cuts in Mercury," BBC News, February 4, 2003, news.bbc.co.uk/1/hi/xci/tech/2722629.stm (Accessed March 3, 2003.)

p. 107, Hulen, Tara. "Dispatch from Toxic Town," *OnEarth Magazine*, Winter 2003, www.nrdc.org/onearth/03in/toxictown1.asp (Accessed March 3, 2003.)

p. 113, Goodman, Peter S. "China Serves As Dump Site For Computers," *Washington Post*, February 24, 2003, p. A01.

p. 113, Goodman.

pp. 114–115, Langewiesche, William. "The Shipbreakers," *The Atlantic* online, August 2000, www.theatlantic.com/issues/2000/08/langewiesche.htm (Accessed March 3, 2003.)

p. 115, Langewiesche.

Chapter Eight
p. 117, "Asphalt and the Jungle," *Economist.com*, July 22, 2004, www.economist.com/PrinterFriendly.cfm?Story_ID=2946928 (Accessed Aug. 12, 2004.)

p. 118, "Hot Potato," *Economist.com*, February 13, 2003, www.economist.com/finance/PrinterFriendly.cfm?Story_ID=1579333 (Accessed March 10, 2003.)

p. 119, "Warm-Up for Climate Debate," *Washington Post*, January 6, 2003, p. A14.

p. 119, "Environment," ChevronTexaco, www.chevrontexaco.com/social_responsibility/environment/ (Accessed December 19, 2002.)

p. 120, Frey, Darcy. "How Green Is BP?" *New York Times*, December 8, 2002, www.nytimes.com/2002/12/08/magazine/088P.html (Accessed March 10, 2003.)

p. 120, Frey.

p. 120, Chang, Kenneth. "As Earth Warms, the Hottest Issue Is Energy," *New York Times*, November 4, 2003, www.nytimes.com/2003/11/04/science/earth/04ENER.html (Accessed Jan. 8, 2004.)

p. 120, Brooks, David. "Clearing the Air," *New York Times*, April 20, 2004, www.nytimes.com/2004/04/20/opinion/20BR00.html

p. 121, Langewiesch.

Conclusion

p. 122, "Summary: Living Planet Report 2002," World Wildlife Fund, July 9, 2002, www.panda.org/news_facts/publications/general/ livingplanet/index.cfm (Accessed March 10, 2003.)

p. 122, Summary.

p. 123, Summary.

p. 123, McNeill, p. 358.

p. 124, Summary.

p. 124, Meadows, p. 278.

Further Information

Further Reading

Burne, David. *Earth Watch*. London: Dorling Kindersley, 2001.

Carson, Rachel. *Silent Spring*. Boston: Houghton Mifflin Company, 1962.

Fridell, Ron. *Global Warming*. New York: Franklin Watts, 2002.

Goodall, Jane, and Marc Bekoff. *The Ten Trusts*. San Francisco: HarperSanFrancisco, 2003.

Silverstein, Alvin. *Food Chains*. Brookfield, CT: Twenty-First Century Books, 1998.

Suzuki, David T., and Holly Dressel. *Good News for a Change*. Vancouver, British Columbia, Canada: Greystone Books, 2003.

Web Sites

These Web sites are good places to pick up information and ideas on the issues discussed in this book.

Environmental Protection Agency (EPA)
www.epa.gov
The U.S. government agency created to protect human health and the environment. This site contains a wide variety of information on the rules and regulations governing the development and conservation of natural resources.

Property and Environment Research Center (PERC)
www.perc.org
A site that gives the free market environmentalist point of view, reporting on free market-style projects for protecting the environment.

Sierra Club
www.sierraclub.org
Site of the nation's oldest and largest environmentalist organization, dedicated to promoting the responsible use of the earth's ecosystems and resources.

United Nations Environment Program (UNEP)
www.unep.org
Site of the U.N. organization devoted to caring for the world's environment. Contains information on various UNEP programs worldwide.

World Bank
lnweb18.worldbank.org/ESSD/envext.nsf/41ByDoc-Name/Environment
Site that outlines current projects for protecting the environment sponsored by this international lending institution.

World Business Council for Sustainable Development (WBCSD)

www.wbcsd.ch

This site reports on activities of businesses around the world designed to promote sustainable development.

Bibliography

Ellis, Richard. *The Empty Ocean: Plundering the World's Marine Life*. Washington, DC: Island Press/Shearwater Books, 2003.

Garretson, Martin S. *The American Bison: The Story of Its Extermination as a Wild Species and Its Restoration Under Federal Protection*. New York: New York Zoological Society, 1938.

Gil, Patricia Robles, editor. *Wilderness: Earth's Last Wild Places*. Washington, DC: Conservation International, 2002.

Goudie, Andrew S, ed. *Encyclopedia of Global Change: Environmental Change and Human Society*. New York: Oxford University Press, 2002.

Hawken, Paul, Amory Lovins and L. Hunter Lovins. *Natural Capitalism: Creating the Next Industrial Revolution*. New York: Little, Brown and Company, 1999.

McNeill, J. R. *Something New Under the Sun: An Environmental History of the Twentieth-Century World*. New York: W. W. Norton & Company, 2000.

Meadows, Donella, Jorgen Randers, and Dennis Meadows. *Limits to Growth*. White River Junction, VT: Chelsea Green Publishing Company, 2004.

Ponting, Clive. *A Green History of the World*. New York: St. Martin's Press, 1991.

Rischard, Jean-Francois. *High Noon: Twenty Global Problems, Twenty Years to Solve Them*. New York: Basic Books, 2002.

Smil, Vaclav. *The Earth's Biosphere: Evolution, Dynamics, and Change*. Cambridge, MA: MIT Press, 2003.

Speth, James Gustave. *Red Sky at Morning: America and the Crisis of the Global Environment*. New Haven, CT: Yale University Press, 2004.

Wilson, Edward O. *The Future of Life*. New York: Alfred A. Knopf, 2002.

Index

Page numbers in **boldface** are illustrations.

Ron Fridell has written for radio, television, newspapers, and textbooks. He has written books on social and political issues, such as terrorism and espionage, and scientific topics, such as DNA fingerprinting and global warming. His most recent book for Marshall Cavendish Benchmark was *Capital Punishment* in the Open for Debate series. He taught English as a second language while a member of the Peace Corp in Bankok, Thailand. He lives in Evanston, Illinois, with his wife Patricia, and his dog, an Australian Shepherd named Madeline.